GOVERNMENT DEPARTMENTS
An organizational perspective

D.C. Pitt and B.C. Smith

ROUTLEDGE DIRECT EDITIONS

ROUTLEDGE & KEGAN PAUL
London, Boston and Henley

For Jean

First published in 1981
by Routledge & Kegan Paul Ltd
39 Store Street,
London WC1E 7DD,
9 Park Street,
Boston, Mass. 02108, USA and
Broadway House,
Newtown Road,
Henley-on-Thames,
Oxon RG9 1EN
Printed in Great Britain by
Thomson Litho Ltd, East Kilbride, Scotland

British Library Cataloguing in Publication Data

Pitt, Douglas C

  Government departments. - (Routledge direct
  editions).
  1. Great Britain - Executive departments
  I. Title   II. Smith, Brian Clive
  354.41   JN451   80 41858

ISBN 0 7100 0742 6

CONTENTS

FIGURES

PREFACE

For some years now we have been teaching public administration and organizational analysis to different groups of students including undergraduates and practising civil servants. We have found much of the traditional public administration literature, including that to which we have contributed, unsatisfactory in that it does not exploit an organizational perspective to the full. It seems paradoxical to us that the most important government agencies are also the most neglected by organization theorists. This book attempts, at an introductory level, to apply concepts from the organizational analysis literature to a group of administrative bodies which are at the heart of the system of government. The central claim of the book is that such an approach can enrich our understanding of the administrative process. Organizational analysis has concentrated heavily on the business firm. While the scope of the discipline has been expanded in recent years to include institutions such as trade unions, hospitals, prisons and voluntary bodies, with notable exceptions organizational studies of the government department are virtually non-existent. This is particularly surprising at a time when students of business organizations are increasingly acknowledging the interdependence of the public and private sectors. The government department clearly deserves the attention of organizational analysts not least because private industry benefits from the inside knowledge of the government machine which distinguished civil servants so often bring to their management boards when they retire.

We hope the book will be of interest to academic students of public administration and organizational theory at degree and diploma levels. We also hope that it will give practising administrators some fresh ideas with which to reinterpret their experience.

We are indebted to Tavistock Publications Limited for permission to use in amended version a diagram which appears in Charles Perrow's 'Organizational Analysis'. Our thanks are due to Gill Speirs for the excellent way in which she typed the manuscript.

INTRODUCTION

In this book we seek to apply some concepts and theories from the
study of organizations in general to the study of British government
departments in the hope that this will not only provide a useful
framework in which existing information on them can be ordered but
also suggest fruitful avenues along which further research might be
carried on. The problem that is encountered immediately one tries
to launch such a project is that organization theory is such a
diverse area of academic activity. Formal organizations have long
been of interest to a wide range of disciplines, each with its own
perspective on the phenomena to be studied. It cannot be said that
the large literature on organizations resembles an ordered state of
knowledge (Silverman, 1970, p.1). Rose believes the 'explosive'
growth in organization theory to be 'one of the most extraordinary
features of contemporary intellectual life' (Rose, 1978, p.18),
resulting in a 'shambles' rather than an integrated theoretical
edifice.
   Nevertheless, the use of this diverse literature seems to us to
offer more insights into the organizations which are our subject
matter than conventional public administration as it has developed
in Britain. Organization theory has begun to make its impact in
the academic study of the public sector, particularly in the field
of local government, but it has not progressed very far. The
government department, perhaps inevitably given the secretive nature
of British central government, has been hardly touched.
   In chapter 1 we explain the advantages which a perspective on
government departments derived from organization theory has over
the more traditional methods of public administration as an area
of academic inquiry. We contrast organizational analysis with the
rather formal and descriptive historical approach of public
administration and with explanations of departments in terms of
constitutional rules and conventions. The advantages of a different
perspective lie in its sensitivity to the complexity of large
organizations. It alerts us to the conflict between the interests
of organizational members which is now regarded as a ubiquitous
feature of organizations. They cannot be regarded as harmonious
collectivities but plural societies. Organization theory thus
corrects the rationalist flaw in much traditional public administra-

1

tion. We argue that managerial problems are better understood from
an organization theory perspective. We point to the advantages
which such theory seems to offer of a distinct, systematic and
precise vocabulary of organizations rather than a language
constrained by the formalities of constitutional argument. This is
of crucial importance if there is to be any comparative study of
organizations, public or private, British or foreign. Organization
theory offers a number of conceptual schemes within which such
comparative analysis might be carried on. In this first chapter
we also offer a number of reasons why government departments deserve
and need the kind of analysis we recommend for them - their
significance for social well-being (or ill), their central position
in the web of government, their economic impact and the power of
the supposedly instrumental and neutral official. Finally, we
introduce the concepts which are central to our subsequent
discussion and around which it is organized.

The variety within organization theory is at once a help and
a hindrance. Organization theorists have developed their ideas
through studies of widely differing organizations to which they
have brought their own sometimes conflicting perspectives.
Organization theory has always been founded on controversy between
the proponents of alternative perceptions of organization. It is
important not to forget the extent to which conflicting methodologies
and even ideological perspectives characterize the field. We have
drawn on concepts and theories in an eclectic fashion as and when
we thought that they would enable us to obtain an improved
perspective on our subject matter. There are undoubtedly modes
of analysis which we have not employed but which readers will feel
have been wrongly omitted. We have certainly not tried to produce
anything like a comprehensive survey of the available theories and
approaches.

Organizational analysis had its origins in attempts to solve
managerial problems about the best way to organize work and the
workplace so as to maximize output, productivity and profits. The
early principles (some would say proverbs) of management and
administration were highly prescriptive, recommending the best way
of running an organization to its owners, managers or leaders.
There is still an important prescriptive element in organizational
thinking, not least in government during the last twenty years or
so. The idea that there is 'one best way' to run any organization
has, however, lost all credibility.

One of the most influential intellectual developments as far as
organization theory is concerned is systems thinking. Its influence
has been felt in many branches of the subject (Silverman, 1970). An
example is the relationship perceived by many theorists between
environmental factors, such as the technology of the productive
process, and organizational structure. Another is the emphasis in
some branches of the subject on the functions which organizations
perform for society and their implications for internal working
arrangements. Systems theory sees organizations as composed of
interdependent parts which adapt to changes in the environment in
order to survive. Here one encounters the problem of reification,
of ascribing 'needs' and 'actions' to organizations independently
of their members. There is also a latent value judgment in the

organizational perceptions of systems theory (as in some of its
other areas of application such as political 'systems'). This is
that the objectives of adjustment and survival appear to be those
of the current beneficiaries of a society. The dominant elements
within the social arrangement portrayed as a system have a more
obvious interest in its survival and adaptation than those exploited
by it. Rose sums up the severe problems of systems theory thus:
'the systems image depends upon logical confusion, unwarranted
practical convenience and ideological thinking' (Rose, 1978, p.245).

In chapter 2 we examine one of the elements in the systems model,
the environment, but more from the point of view of the conflicting
demands placed upon organizations by their environments than the
possibilities of adjustment to some systems equilibrium by way of
homeostatic mechanisms. We survey briefly the environmental
conditions said to be significant to organizations and place
particular emphasis on the political and legal context of government
departments. This we characterize in terms of values operationalized
through institutions. This view is not only consistent with the
importance which is attached to the political setting of government
administration. It also squares with the emphasis placed in
government on the integration of institutions so that government
works to a certain extent as a single mechanism in a way that is
not expected of private organizations (Parker and Subramaniam, 1964).
We see the environment of government departments as consisting of a
network of other institutions each attempting to enforce its
dominant value on the administrative process. The environment may
also therefore be considered in inter-organizational terms. We
consider this possibility, together with the important qualification
that organizations should not be regarded as totally subservient to
environmental influences. The values which we consider - accountability, efficiency, legality, consultation, fairness and reasonableness - and their concomitant institutions should not just be seen
as constraints imposed by the expectations channelled from the
political community. Values and departments interact through the
medium of the institutions which represent those values. We
indicate here how the environment of the department has implications,
not only for its administrative and managerial processes, but also
for its structure and goals, the subjects of later chapters.

A concern to find the best way to run an organization prompts
the question 'best for what and for whom?' It assumes some goal
which should be maximized using resources in the most effective and
efficient way. But whose goals? It is no longer thought appropriate
to speak of the goals of organizations themselves, though an
important strand in organizational analysis has been the conceptualization of organizations in terms of their goal-seeking purpose. This
carries with it all the attendant risks of reification: 'the
attribution of concrete reality, particularly the power of thought
and action to social constructs' (Silverman, 1970). Nevertheless,
the importance of goal analysis should not be underestimated, least
of all in the study of government departments where political goals
of the leadership (ministers) may be in conflict with the formal
goals of the organization (statutory powers).

In chapter 3 we discuss the utility of goal analysis. The
necessity for this arises from the implication of rationality which

resides in the very concept of organization. We show the inappropri-
ateness of regarding governmental goals as being solely formulated
by agencies external to the departments of state and reject a formal
model of policy-making which rests on a distinction between politics
and administration or policy-making and policy implementation. The
factors which lead members of departments to be considered as goal-
setters are discussed. We also apply the concepts of goal conflict,
goal displacement and goal succession. We place considerable
emphasis on the relationship between the multiplicity of goals which
departments generate and the conflicting interests which reside
within departments as in all large, complex, formal organizations.

We also consider in chapter 3 the question of informal goals and
the place in organization theory for the possibility of goal conflict
arising between the formal goals of the organization and the private
goals of individuals and groups within it. We relate what is known
about the attitudes of civil servants towards their work to the
assumptions that lie behind some of the changes that have been
introduced into government in recent years, particularly in the form
of accountable management.

The structural attributes of formal organizations have long been
of central concern to organization theorists of different methodological persuasions and have been a source of controversy within
the field since Weber's conceptualization of bureaucracy (1947).
The study of formal organizational structures has arranged itself
around the bureaucratic model, partly to test the advantages claimed
for it and partly to show how far some organizations find it
appropriate to deviate considerably from bureaucratic principles.

A preoccupation with formal structure was rectified by industrial
psychologists and sociologists who emphasized the importance of
informal social structures in the workplace. This approach analysed
the workforce in terms of human needs and motivations in a social
setting. They rejected the model of man as an isolated,
materialistic automaton, constrained in the pursuit of rewards only
by physical and physiological limitations. So an important branch
of organization theory has focused on the significance of small,
informal work-groups; the needs of individuals not only for
acceptance but also for self-fulfilment; the social costs of technical
efficiency, and the relationship between individual needs and
organizational interests. Many theoretical problems have been
raised: how do we validate the existence of 'needs'? How can
informal and formal structures be integrated? Is a concern for
needs just another manipulative, exploitative device? Does it
underestimate the importance of economic motives and extra-
organizational factors for work? Do needs really explain behaviour?
Social psychologists have made a major contribution to our knowledge
of organizational life by drawing attention to the potential for
conflict between the needs of individuals and the goals of
organizations, unless those goals are expressed simply in terms of
individuals' objectives.

We take up the issue of structure in chapter 4 and concentrate on
the question of the relationship, if any, between structure and the
successful performance of organizational tasks. We examine the
elements of departmental structure with particular reference to the
variations to be found between departments. A number of theoretical

conceptualizations are considered which have been employed by
organization theorists interested in the structural attributes of
successful organizations. The applicability of such concepts to the
government department is evaluated. We pay particular attention to
the contingency approach to organizations and consider the usefulness
of Perrow's adaptation of 'technology' to non-industrial settings for
our own purposes in examining the tasks of government departments
and relating those tasks to structural configurations. We conclude
this chapter with some consideration of the weaknesses of contingency
theory, and in particular those which show up when it is applied to
government departments. We attach special importance to the idea of
strategic choice between organizational alternatives and the role of
internal political factors in the way in which organizations respond
to technology and environment.

A perspective on organisations which stresses the significance of
conflicts of interest over choices made within them owes much to a
major alternative to systems thinking, namely the action approach to
sociological phenomena (Silverman, 1970). Here the focus of
attention is on the relationship between the active involvement of
members in their organizations and their social values or 'definitions
of the situation'. Silverman, for example, argues that the important
features of organizations are the meanings given by people in them
to roles and actions and the origins and consequences of conflicts
between these meanings and perceptions. It is the relationships
subjectively perceived and defined by participants which are
important rather than those of 'objective' outsiders.

Action theory is a perspective which suggests that organizational
structure is to a degree the result of individual actions and
choices. Thus viewed, organizational reality is not totally external
to individuals. It is partly defined by their values and behaviour.
Action theory is thus a corrective to system theories which reify
structure and see it as having an existence independent of the
individuals who occupy it.

One of the central controversies in contemporary organization
theory is in fact between those who emphasize power and conflict
within organizations and those who emphasize the impact of situational
contingencies on various aspects of organizations, particularly
structure. This latter approach overlaps with some of the off-shoots
of systems theory. It is adopted by a school of analysts who apply
quantitative techniques to variations in the relationship between
organizational factors such as size and structural configurations
(Pugh et al., 1968 and 1969). This approach utilizes totally
different data and forms of explanation from the action approach,
attempting as it does to emulate natural science by regarding social
behaviour as comprehensible by the same methods of understanding as
the behaviour of matter. Action theorists question whether an
external logic can be applied to human behaviour in organizations,
or anywhere else, in the way that natural scientists impose a frame
of reference and therefore meaning on the physical world, though
they share the same concern that procedures of investigation and
analysis should be systematic and rigorous.

Action theory, however, is not without its own problems,
particularly in its conceptualization of power. It is unlikely that
the power of individuals or groups will only depend on the perceptions

of the dominant and subordinate elements in the relationship, unless they are merely engaged in a propaganda battle. Power depends on objective factors. More often than not a power relationship will depend on the resources which people actually possess, rather than on what they believe they possess. An effective exercise of power need not be dependent on a 'definition' of a situation which modifies someone else's perception of it. It may simply be a question of who has the more coercive ability. Imposing one's definition of the situation will often be a consequence, not a cause, of power: 'the power holder does not need to modify a subordinate's perceptions to have his way' (Rose, 1978, p.247). There is also the question of whether, in taking a participant's definition of roles, actions and consequences into account, we should accept this as the final explanation. If we do, we are in danger of being left with the chaotic relativity of subjective rationalities (Rose, 1978, p.248).

Conflicting perceptions of organizational goals, objectives and administrative processes should not be overlooked or ignored, however, though it is surprisingly easy for this to happen. In our chapter on management in government departments (chapter 5) we examine the tendency in recent years to adopt an approach to organizational problems which sees issues of structure and process as unproblematic. In particular it assumes consensus on the need for prescribed changes. We examine the impact of a 'managerialist' philosophy in British central government which emerged through a growing interest in the applicability to departments of managerial techniques which it was believed had been successful in the private sector. In this context, we outline the background to the Fulton inquiry and its aftermath. We argue that any set of management principles must take into account the distinctive features of departmental management such as the absence of measures of profitability and the consequent problem of establishing levels of efficiency; the impact of the political environment and the importance to be attached to it; and the imperative of equity. We show how these distinctive features led to a style of management which conflicted with the values of reformers. We stress that changes in departmental organization have, however, taken place in response to this managerialist critique. We describe the structural changes to the civil service that have been made and the new methods of management that have been introduced. We point as well to the disturbance which such change generates and the consequent resistance which it provokes among organizational participants. This raises the question of the power resources which interests may mobilize to defend the status quo.

Power and the effectiveness of different modes of command, direction and control have always been central themes in organization theory. Power is reflected to a certain extent in the formal organization chart. This was a pre-occupation of early theorists. In addition, of course, power relationships exist outside the formal chain of command and as such have become of major interest to more recent theorists. Etzioni, for example, has classified organizations according to the type of power relationship which they exist to provide. He argues that compliance may be obtained by coercion (as in a prison), remuneration (as in an office) or appeals to moral norms (as in a priesthood). So compliance may be characterized by alienation, bargaining or moral commitment. This gives the possibility of nine 'pure' types of organization, some more likely in practice than others (Etzioni, 1961). Crozier (1964) has shown that the formal organization, at least in a bureaucratic system, may yet be important. It reduces uncertainty. In work-groups, to be uncertain about what others will do is a position of weakness, leading to power conflicts.

Such concerns with power as these have led to yet another departure in organization theory, away from a unitary view of organizations and towards a pluralistic conception of them as consisting of competing interests (Fox, 1966). 'Recognition of power and status systems within organizations is a preliminary to the development of a political perspective on organizations which recognizes that they may be sensibly viewed, at least in part, as manifesting divergent interests' (Pitt, 1980, p.13). A pluralistic perspective is a natural extension of the action approach. It builds conflict into the analysis, a factor neglected by earlier schools of thought, especially 'scientific management' and even 'human relations' (Rose, 1978). It also extends the 'technological imperatives' approach by linking conflict to 'situational constraints' such as the technology employed by an organization. Not only will the degree of conflict or co-operation between groups, particularly management and unions, be influenced by such constraints. The structure of authority and the technology employed will themselves be the subject of bargaining and negotiation.

We illustrate this with a case study of the Post Office (chapter 6) which, as an organization that was formerly a department and has latterly become a semi-autonomous organization, is particularly useful for examining pressures for change and the responses which such pressures draw from organizational participants. The relocation of the functions of a government department in a hived-off agency exemplifies the impact of demands for the replacement of a mechanistic departmental structure by a more organic form which would strengthen a commercial approach to its services and which was thought to be more easily achieved in a government organization with the status of a public corporation. There is a long history of attempts to effect such a structural change within the context of the departmental form. We trace the inexorable logic of transformation which has resulted in a change of constitutional status. This case enables us to examine the ideas contained in earlier chapters in relation to a specific institution and so draw together the threads of organizational analysis in a practical context. We show how the new form of organization for the Post Office reflected managerialist thinking and how this thinking developed in the context of conflict between interests and values. These arose from the internal division of labour within the Post Office and external political factors.

Finally, in chapter 7, we consider the demise of consensus politics and of the managerialism associated with it. We examine some of the alternatives which have been proposed to bureaucratic organizations: reducing the functions of government; strengthening the moral purpose of public administration; and abandoning bureaucracy or even organizations generally. We suggest that a political perspective on organizations reveals that such proposals will be extremely difficult to implement and may be objectionable in a democratic society.

Organization theorists have attempted to apply the fruits of a wide range of disciplines to organizational life. Their approaches have produced an amazing variety of interpretations. As this work has moved from an almost exclusive concern with industrial organizations to other kinds (prisons, welfare institutions, hospitals, military units and so on), it has gained strength from the varied perspectives brought to bear (Silverman, 1970, p.3). What stands out when an attempt is made to apply some of these approaches to specific organizations is the integrated nature of organizational life. It is artificial to separate out goals, environment, structure, management and so on (though the current state of knowledge as far as government departments are concerned forces us to), since in the daily operations of any formal organization all these elements interrelate. The environment has implications for structure. Structure in turn impinges on goals (through, for example, goal displacement). Management can be conceived of in part as having a responsibility for both goals and structure. It is not possible to understand fully one feature of organization in isolation from the others.

An eclectic approach seems intrinsically advantageous and indeed inevitable until a more integrated theory is available. We take encouragement from W.J.M. Mackenzie's description of organization theory as a 'sequence of schools gradually enriching thought' and as a field 'in which all sorts of inconsistent theories survive together, for the good reason that no single theory is necessarily the best theory even for a single situation' (Mackenzie, 1967, p.246).

THE GOVERNMENT DEPARTMENT AND ORGANIZATIONAL ANALYSIS

In choosing to write about the government department as an organization we are, in effect, making two assertions which need to be justified in this first chapter. One is that the study of administrative institutions in government needs to employ methods of analysis which have rarely been used in the field of orthodox public administration. These methods are drawn from organization theory and, in the main, have been applied to firms in the private sector rather than public sector organizations. In so far as organization theory has drawn upon data from the public sector it has tended to look to specialized public institutions which are in many respects remote from the centres of political conflict and influence which ultimately dominate the organizations of the modern state. Such institutions have included schools, hospitals, universities and welfare agencies. Only recently has organization theory been applied even to local government. The nationalized industries have also been relatively neglected, surprisingly in view of what organization theory owes to the study of industrial organizations. Our second assertion is simply that the government department is a sufficiently important organization to warrant separate treatment in its own right.

AN ORGANIZATIONAL PERSPECTIVE

First, then, there is the question of method. Public administration as an area of study has tended to be legalistic and descriptive. It has drawn heavily on law, history and traditional political studies for its disciplinary bases. Central government departments (and the same could be said, though happily to a lesser extent recently, of local government departments) have been studied as elements in the machinery of government with the emphasis on the constitutional relationships between parliament, the courts, ministers and the civil service whose members constitute the personnel of central departments. Formal descriptions of ministries and departments have occasionally been written, but as official statements of purpose and structure rather than analytical studies of social phenomena. A good example of this genre is the 'Whitehall' series of books on

individual departments (for example, Bridges, 1964 and Sharp, 1969).
Accounts of formal hierarchies and the tasks of individual units in
terms of the statutory powers of ministers provide only the barest
outline of the organizational complexity of government departments.
For the organization theorist such information is but the first
stage of an inquiry which asks questions about informal social roles
and structures within complex organizations; about the relationships
between organizational structure and factors upon which this is
contingent, such as size, technology and the nature of the tasks to
be performed; about the effect of an organization's environment on
its operations; and about the goals which are the raison d'etre of
formal organization. An organizational perspective is also more
dynamic in that it is concerned with the process of change and its
origins, giving a more realistic account of organizations as social
structures in which bargaining, negotiation and conflict over goals
and structure are universal.

Alternatively, political scientists interested in the study of
administrative and executive processes in government have restricted
themselves to the problem of power. This is an issue with both
political and constitutional dimensions, and the analysis has
tended to focus on the nature and legitimacy of the power of
officials in a political system which in theory relegates the
bureaucrat to a purely instrumental role as the paid servant of
the elected politician. Inevitably such an orientation is towards
the minority of senior officials in the administrative hierarchy
who can be regarded as policy-makers. Again the focus of interest
is the relationships between institutions - in this case the
relative power of official and unofficial groups, such as senior
civil servants, ministers, MPs and organized interests. Consequently,
public administration as an area of study, heavily influenced by
political science, has tended to neglect the practice of administering in the sense which is synonymous with organizing, managing or
just 'getting things done' in favour of administration in the sense
which is rather peculiar to central government departments, namely
policy advice and analysis in support of ministers' political roles.
Thus public administrationists have been preoccupied with the factors
which distinguish public from private organizations, namely their
political settings, while organization theorists are more interested
in the problems common to all organizations, public or private,
social or economic, although by no means believing that the same
statements can be made about all of them.

Organization theory has generally approached public organizations,
such as central or local government departments, as a species within
the genus 'organization'. They are not assumed a priori to constitute
a separate generic category requiring a quite separate methodology.
Their public status may be an important explanatory factor, but
what it explains are organizational attributes likely to be found
in all organizations, public or private. So public organizations
can be compared with private by reference to a common set of concepts
and hypotheses. For example, their dependence on, or subordination
to, other organizations can be compared. The nature of public goals
and the evaluation of performance are other common reference points,
as is the range of tasks performed by public agencies. The academic
study of public administration, on the other hand, has tended to

assume that public organizations are, because of their public position, sufficiently distinct to warrant not only separate treatment, but also an exclusive conceptual and methodological approach (Hinings and Greenwood, 1973).

One of the commonest assumptions in public administration is that the peculiar requirements of public accountability produce distinctive organizational traits in government agencies such as ministerial departments. 'On the basis of the classical literature on bureaucracy as a societal phenomenon, it might be hypothesized that organizations with the greatest exposure to public accountability would have a higher degree of structuring of activities, and a greater concentration of authority' (Pugh et al., 1968). Comparative research, however, reveals a rather more complicated picture.

The Aston research, for example, found no relationship between public accountability and the 'structuring of activities' (i.e. the degree to which employee behaviour is overtly defined by task specialization, standard routines and formal paperwork). This was the case with both the 'workflow' and administrative activities of the government organizations in the sample, and it appeared that 'government organizations with a workflow are not differentiated from non-government organizations on this basis' (Pugh et al., 1968). However, there was found to be a positive relationship between public accountability and the 'concentration of authority' (i.e. 'the degree to which authority for decisions rests in controlling units outside the organization and is centralized at the higher hierarchical levels within it'). Public accountability was also found to centralize authority, increase the level of standardization in procedures for selection and promotion, and increase the extent to which control is exercised by line personnel instead of impersonal procedures.

From evidence such as this, it seems that we cannot predict that public accountability will produce a standard bureaucratic pattern of organization. Furthermore, we may have to differentiate between parts of bodies such as ministerial departments. The administrative activities in, for example, the headquarters divisions of departments may require structures which are themselves susceptible to different contextual influences than the 'workflow' activities of branches, sections, and local offices.

Organization analysis offers a number of advantages over more conventional attempts to explain public sector institutions, sensitizing us to the problems of organization in ways in which public administration has not.

First, it offers the possibility of comparative studies, not only across countries but also across categories of organization which can only be dealt with as unique, and therefore descriptively, by the old style of approach to government institutions. This possibility arises from the conceptual apparatus provided by organization theories which are not tied to any particular class of organization. There is, for example, the Weberian conceptualization of bureaucracy which Blau and Scott claim to be 'the most important general statement on formal organization' (Blau and Scott, 1963, p.27). Weber's concept of legal or rational authority is of particular significance in the context of modern government characterized by the bureaucratic form of administration which accompanies the legitimacy attached to impersonal rules.

Alternatively, it may prove fruitful to employ the general theoretical framework of Talcott Parsons and so regard organizations as social systems which, as such, must solve the problems of adaptation, goal achievement, integration and latency. We can learn much about government departments by asking how they adapt to their environments, how they seek to achieve their objectives, how they integrate and co-ordinate their separate parts, and how they promote the legitimacy of their activities (Parsons, 1960). It should be noted, however, that contemporary organization theory takes more account of conflict and the clash of interests that characterizes the social system of organization than did functionalists such as Parsons. Many organization theorists have concentrated on the third function of integration and have developed conceptual frameworks for analysing the internal structure of organizations. For example, Burns and Stalker (1961), whose work we shall refer to again, distinguish between organic and mechanistic structures in order to relate the integrating arrangements of successful firms to the context of changing objectives and technology within which they operate. Other theorists wishing to relate structural characteristics to other variables such as size, technology of production, goals and social setting employ a conceptualization of structure for comparative purposes such as that developed by the Aston University project: functional specialization, role specialization, standardization, formalization, centralization and line versus procedural controls (Pugh et al., 1969).

There are many other conceptual schemes, typologies and classifications that have been developed to facilitate comparative analysis. It is a matter of deciding which serves the purposes of the analyst best. It may even be thought necessary to separate private from public organizations. There is a good deal of debate about the wisdom of this which we refer to later. But even if this is done, the resulting classification is still likely to be based on organizational rather than constitutional distinctions if it is to be of value as a tool of comparative analysis. The public/private distinction may be a useful explanatory variable, for example, in asking what effect public or private ownership has on the management of a hospital, industry or school. But implicit in this is a wider organizational framework of dependent and independent variables of which state ownership is but one. If this variable is elevated to a classification it can only impede analysis by asserting a priori that public organizations are different from private. It would also, if taken to its logical extreme, prevent a comparison of similar institutions, such as hospitals and schools, in the public and private spheres.

This leads to the second advantage of organization theory. If we wish to talk about organizations in a distinctive way, we need a language for it. The languages of other disciplines - political science, sociology and psychology for example - are not enough to identify and analyse the distinctively organizational attributes of the various forms of life and action with which they are concerned. Although social, economic and political activities are carried on through organizations and influenced by them, the disciplines that make those activities their subject matter do not provide a common language in which to analyse the organizational aspects of different spheres of life. Nowhere is this more obvious than in the study of public administration. In the United Kingdom it has suffered from being forced into the categories and language of constitutional history and political science, just as in the United States it used to be constrained by the language of management, its parent discipline. This is why, until relatively recently, we find the study of public organization fragmented into the study of categories which correspond to constitutional distinctions (central departments, nationalized industries and local authorities, for example), and dominated by a 'machinery of government' approach which focused almost exclusively on the interrelationships between institutions - ministers and civil servants; parliament and the executive; departments and local authorities; and so on. Organizational issues were screened out by the selective bias engendered by the dominant mode of discourse in public administration. Hence 'the usefulness of developing a distinct, systematic and precise vocabulary of organization' (Bradley and Wilkie, 1974, p.19).

Neither of the foregoing points imply that any statement about organizations will necessarily apply to all types - schools as well as hospitals, police forces as well as electronics firms. Indeed, an organization theory perspective should help us to become aware of the complexities and variations to be observed in organizations of a single type. As Perrow has observed after contrasting two correctional institutions, 'within the same "type" of organization - in this case a "people - changing institution" - a wide variety of techniques, structures, and goals can be used' (Perrow, 1970, p.36). Perrow uses this conclusion to warn against packaged remedies for organizational problems - the idea that there is a standard set of principles guaranteeing good administration in any context. This idea is now generally rejected by theoreticians though, as Perrow says,

many business and government consulting services come equipped with neat packages of nostrums. Not surprisingly they find that every organization they advise needs just what is in their package, whether it be a better data-processing system, linear programming, human relations programmes or executive development programmes, better control techniques, or a better marketing system. (Perrow, 1970, p.37)

This warning is particularly appropriate to a consideration of central government departments. Proposals for administrative and political reform have tended to regard departments as uniform. Recently, Hood, Dunsire and Thompson have questioned 'the usefulness of "blanket" proposals for reform ... given that departments can be shown to differ widely from one another in structure, context and type of work' (1979). Having 'run the ruler over Whitehall' they found no standard pattern. Civil service departments vary enormously in size as well as in their structural shape and complexity as measured by concentrations of different grades of staff, the numerical significance of generalists, and the proportion of headquarters, as distinct from field, staff. These findings deal with only a few of the possible dimensions of structure, but do enough to justify their authors' cautious handling of prescriptions to design or redesign better government agencies by reference to general principles, at least before the range of variation in existing departments has been ascertained and understood.

One aspect of organization which the formalistic approach to public administration barely hints at, but which is a central theme in organizational theory, is the significance of the informal social structures and relationships which develop whenever people come together within the formal structure of organizations. There is a long (and chequered) history of theoretical and empirical concern with networks of human relations in industrial organizations, the impact of group subcultures on work and the connecting links between the formal organization and work-groups (Blau and Scott, 1963, ch.4). The field has been dominated by industrial sociology with all its attendant defects of methodology and ideological bias (Rose, 1978). However, enough is now known about social relationships within organizations to avoid thinking of them as harmonious units. The plurality of groups and interests into which organizations may be divided makes it no longer possible to think of organizations as having the characteristics of individuals – intentions, goals, purposes, needs, actions, interests, objectives and ends. Different members will have different ends. An organization will encompass a plurality of interests, not all of which will be compatible with those of the senior executives or the intentions of the founding fathers. An organization will often appear to 'pursue' a variety of ends which may conflict with each other. The formal structure, as reflected in organization charts and manuals, will only give part of the picture of communication and control. Different individuals in an organization will find their needs satisfied in different ways and to different degrees by membership of it. Different levels of motivation, satisfaction and involvement will be produced by experience of the organization. Organizations should not be reified as systems or organic unities. We refer to this again in the chapters on goals and structure.

Having said that, there is still no denying that organizations are created to achieve the goals of people who could not achieve them without the co-ordination of individuals' actions implied by the existence of organizations. The question of the rationality, efficiency and effectiveness of an organization is a meaningful one. It need not lead us to reify the organization or deny that only some of its members will have an interest in its efficiency or that other members will judge what the organization is doing in terms of their own ends and therefore their own rationality. The importance of organization theory here is twofold. First, it has been concerned with how the structural and behavioural characteristics of organizations may be related to success, however that may be measured. Initially there was a widespread belief that the application of a universal set of principles would guarantee organizational success. This was descredited theoretically (notably by Herbert Simon) and empirically (notably by Joan Woodward), but organization theorists still demonstrated an interest in whether one form of organization was more likely than another to help achieve success, given the circumstances in which the organization found itself. Such circumstances, or contingencies, arose mainly from the market environment of the firm or the technology of its production process. Organization theory has been interested in the implications of technology for both worker morale and management structures, but ultimately for organizational performance –

productivity, return on investment, profitability, share of the market and so on. As far as organizational structures are concerned, theorists have become increasingly interested in whether by matching structure to environment an organization can be made to work better.

The other reason why organization theory is important in this context is that some theorists have drawn our attention to the fact that rationalistic approaches to organization must serve someone's interests. Usually changes are considered by managers and owners as ways of furthering their interests in profits. Organizational change is seen as a means of securing worker compliance. It is important to be aware that management is a manipulative device that may well further the 'goals' of the organization - as perceived by selected individuals or groups within it. There may be no consensus in those goals, and therefore the devices for achieving them may not attract the degree of support which at first glance they seem to deserve. Observations of British government departments suggest that organizational changes, such as merging and dividing departments, introducing new planning techniques like Programme Analysis and Review, creating new lines of command by integrating generalists and specialists and delegating authority down the line to budgetary centres or commands, may threaten as many interests as they promote. Once again the importance of not reifying the organization is obvious.

Nevertheless, it is inevitable that some members of organizations in general, and government departments in particular, will be concerned to improve performance. In government considerable efforts have been made in recent years to create an analytical foundation for this, so that 'output' can be quantified and costed, objectives measured, programmes evaluated and meaningful statements made about whether policies have achieved what was intended at the planned cost. Organization theory, in all its diversity, has offered some valuable insights into the factors relating to certain conceptions of success as well as some salutary cautions about interpretations of organizational change and manipulation.

The foregoing references to organization theory are far from doing justice to its variety or the subtlety of the critiques which it has attracted. We have not attempted the impossible task (for us) of giving a complete survey of organizational studies and theories. Rather, we have tried to identify a few areas of enquiry where an organization theory approach, provided it is properly conscious of its limitations, seems superior to the traditional methods of British public administration when it comes to under-standing public sector organizations.

An organizational perspective of a government department, then, starts from the belief that the sociology of organizations will raise questions which hitherto have not been raised and will lead to aspects of the organization concerned being studied rather than ignored. It will put existing knowledge to better use by arranging it systematically in a structure of ideas whose purpose is to explain rather than describe. It will provide a more complete understanding of the workings of a department, its structure and functioning. It treats the department as problematic and so makes it possible to ask if the appropriate structures have been created and appropriate decision-making processes instituted.

THE IMPORTANCE OF GOVERNMENT DEPARTMENTS

Before justifying our second assertion - that it is important to
have the more complete understanding of government departments just
referred to - we need to make clear precisely what organization we
have in mind as the subject of our analysis. Many governmental
institutions, especially local authorities and public corporations,
label the constituent parts of their administrative or managerial
structures 'departments'. We are not concerned with these, but
with their counterparts in central government and variously known as
'ministries' (for example, Ministry of Defence, Ministry of
Agriculture, Fisheries and Food) or just 'department' (for example,
Department of the Environment, Department of Energy). The variation
in title simply reflects the status of the minister at the head and
we will refer to this group of organizations collectively as
'departments' even though the titles of individual departments may
contain the words 'Ministry', 'Office' (for example, Home Office),
'Board' (for example, Board of Inland Revenue) or none of these
(for example, the Treasury). There are approximately seventy major
and minor departments which together make up the central administration (and are sometimes referred to simply as 'Whitehall'). Each
is headed by a member of 'Her Majesty's Government', who may or may
not be in the Cabinet. Their formal organizational features are
very similar and they are staffed by civil servants. Constitutionally,
their tasks are to implement the policies of their ministers as
derived from parliamentary enactment.
    Why are government departments important subjects for organiza-
tional analysis? First, there is their significance for society
as measured by the scope of functions and services which are
directly or indirectly under their control. It is in the departments
of state that policies are formulated and sometimes directly
implemented for the extensive public intervention in social and
economic affairs. The regulatory state, requiring the public
provision of armed forces, police, courts and prisons has given way
to the interventionist (welfare or redistributive) state, involving
the provision of public goods such as social security, housing,
education and health, and the management of the national economy
in pursuit of welfare or redistributive objectives. The scope of
the modern British state is very broad indeed. It ranges from
deficiency payments to the agriculture industry to the construction
of motorways; from the maintenance of prisons to aerospace research
and development; from the provision of maternity services to the
payment of death grants; from support to bus operators to the
building of Concorde. No mere list can adequately convey the
extent or complexity of the state's role in contemporary society
and its pursuit of public goods. What is important to remember is
that these matters are organized within government departments.
Directly or indirectly, what they do affects nearly every aspect
of the lives of ordinary people. Whether this state of affairs is
desirable is more a question of political philosophy than organizational theory, though values about state intervention inevitably
enter into the thinking of the members of these organizations,
politicians and officials alike. The welfare state and the managed
economy are not matters on which anyone can remain entirely neutral,

and it is sheer mythology to believe that this does not apply to senior civil servants.

An extension of this aspect of the government department's significance is that ultimately all the other agencies of the state with which we come into contact as citizens are subject to varying degrees of supervision and control by the central departments. We may buy our electricity or gas from public corporations, but their investment decisions and pricing policies are made under the powerful influence of government ministers. Local authorities may provide educational institutions, personal social services, traffic schemes, police and fire services, but they are subject to central control, via government departments, on a wide range of matters and often in considerable detail. The departments thus constitute part of the environment within which all public authorities operate, whether they be schools, universities, hospitals, nationalized industries or the police.

The same is true for many private concerns which may be sponsored or constrained by public policy. Farmers may receive production grants and subsidies. Industry is subject to the health and safety inspectorates of central government. The employers of low paid labour are subject to minimum wage agreements enforced by the Department of Employment. The last two examples reveal the significance of official values in that a very small number of prosecutions have actually been pursued against offenders under the relevant statutes. Again, not all private concerns deal continuously with the central government. A factory owner may be prosecuted for pollution by a water authority, for example. But it is unlikely that the policies of that authority have been formulated without guidance from the relevant department.

Third, there is the economic impact of the decisions taken within central departments. They spend or, to varying degrees, control a total public expenditure of around £60,000 million. This accounts for just over 40 per cent of the gross domestic product. They employ 700,000 civil servants or nearly 3 per cent of the total working population. Since these organizations are, as we have seen, in command of the whole public sector they can be said to be in some degree responsible for the impact of the public sector on the economy. This sector not only absorbs more than half of the GNP. It contributes over 40 per cent of all new investment, employs 27 per cent of the working population, pays 32 per cent of all wages and salaries and owns 44 per cent of fixed assets.

Through ultimate control of the public sector and widespread intervention in the private sector the organizations of central government attempt to manage the mixed economy. They attempt to manage the level of demand for real resources, and their distribution between consumption, investment and exports, by controlling public expenditure, by influencing private demand through transfer payments, grants and subsidies, and by varying the rates and types of taxation. Controls are also used to reduce disparities in regional rates of economic growth and employment opportunities.

So far we have referred to 'departments' as homogeneous collectivities. But they contain in their personnel an important distinction to which we have alluded and which is a further reason for subjecting them to organizational analysis. This distinction is between politician and paid official. While political scientists have, as we suggested above, rightly pointed to the importance of ministerial/civil service power relations, organizational theory can enhance this perspective by viewing them as part of a much wider network of power relationships involving groups throughout departments involved in the stipulation and attainment of organizational goals and objectives. Part of the interest and importance of government departments lies in the fact that the constitutional role assigned by our laws and conventions to civil servants is not a complete statement of their power, particularly in their senior ranks. The conventions state that senior civil servants should be non-political. While it is probably true that this is maintained in the sense that officials in government departments serve their ministers with equal loyalty and neutrality regardless of the minister's party, it does not mean that they are powerless. The official's duties include giving advice on public policy options. This advice is proferred from positions of authority based on professional knowledge and experience. Many of the decisions taken by administrators are also initiated by them. They cannot be regarded as the mere instruments of implementation at the disposal of ministers. Policy-making does not divide into the neat categories of ends and means, with administrators confined to devising the means to ends which are laid down by their political masters. Policies themselves are the means to social goals and objectives which are often ill-defined if at all. In the choice of policies the administrator is often in a far more powerful position than the untrained, transient minister preoccupied with political responsibilities and problems outside the department.

Not surprisingly, then, concern is expressed from time to time that the highest ranks of the civil service constitute not only a powerful elite, but also one whose relatively privileged social background will unavoidably introduce a degree of class bias into the policy recommendations which they can present to ministers. To social scientists, conscious of the power enjoyed by different classes in society, the social structure of the civil service is yet further evidence of middle-class domination. Whether one regards the civil service as part of the ruling class or as the servants of representative governments, their influence on political decisions cannot be disputed. Hence it is important to apply the analysis of organizational goals to government departments to see how far organizational behaviour conflicts with the constitutional model of relationships between politicians and administrators. An overemphasis on the constitutional model of the administrative process can lead to departments being regarded as simply the agencies through which political decisions taken elsewhere in the system of government are translated into action. Here the only problems are managerial, a view which has been reinforced by the fasionable wave of managerialism which has swept through Whitehall in recent years. We believe that such an approach diverts attention away from the department as an autonomous source of power in the decision-making process. It downgrades the department as an organization and ignores its potential for generating goals of its own. While many important managerial questions can and should be asked about the means by which policy can be implemented, we must avoid the managerialist fallacy of regarding policy-making as politics and therefore a separate process from administration. Administration within departmental organizations is an integral part of the political process.

This is where organization theory and political theory interrelate. It is the age-old conflict between democracy and bureaucracy in the sense of government by officials. Democratic political theory is normative and prescribes an instrumental role for the paid officials of the state, reserving policy choices for the elected representatives of the people. Organization theory, on the other hand, is positive and postulates that the power of officials enables them to perform a role which is far from subservient. The response to this discrepancy between fact and value may be to recast political theory or search for alternative organizations which are capable of being brought under democratic control. So far in Britain neither course has been found necessary, perhaps because of the power of the prevailing myths about the responsiveness of government organizations. Indeed the political culture permits the creation of more rather than less autonomous bureaucratic organizations within the machinery of government under the powerful influence of managerial values. Concern about the bureaucratization of government is a minority interest. It has been associated with demands for the devolution of power, but even here the main motivating force has been the geographical remoteness of political institutions from the Celtic fringe rather than the conflict between bureaucracy and democracy per se.

None of this should obscure the fact that government departments like other organizations have to perform managerial functions. There are functions in relation to stores, purchasing and contracts. Staff have to be recruited, trained, deployed and motivated. Work has to be planned, organized, controlled and reviewed. Accounts have to be kept and budgets drawn up. New techniques of management have to be introduced. Sometimes these managerial tasks, in terms of the number of staff involved and the techniques of management employed, are comparable to those performed in industry. Sometimes they are not (we explain how and why in a later chapter). Herein lies our final reason for claiming that government departments need organizational analysis. The significance of their decisions for the public welfare is such that their administrative structures and processes must be capable of producing the highest level of efficiency possible. As organizations the public interest demands that they are well managed.

The problem here is one of relating structure and process to task. Organization theory enables a number of common fallacies to be avoided. One is that principles of management found appropriate in private business concerns are transplantable into government departments. Another is that these departments can be treated as a homogeneous group. The fact is that they encompass within and between them a bewildering array of tasks, some of which have their counterparts in the private sector, such as financial planning and accounting, and some of which do not, such as processing planning appeals or regulating consumer credit or environmental pollution. Devising organizational structures appropriate for the tasks to be performed can only be done from an organization theory perspective. One of our tasks in this book is to suggest how such an exercise might be carried out.

We have sought to justify the adoption of an organization theory approach to government departments. We now turn to the central concepts involved in such an approach. These are environment, goals, structure and management. Each of these concepts and their families of related concepts are the material from which theories of organizational behaviour are built up. In the following chapters we deal with each of these concepts in turn in our attempt to explore the organizational life of government departments.

Chapter 2

THE ORGANIZATIONAL ENVIRONMENT OF THE GOVERNMENT DEPARTMENT

The study of organizations soon reveals that they do not exist in a vacuum. What they do is related to the environment within which they exist. It is difficult to generalize about the environments of organizations, because they vary according to the nature of the organization concerned - whether they are privately or publicly owned productive enterprises, educational institutions, professional bodies, voluntary associations, welfare organizations and so on.

Part of the reason for studying the environment of organizations is simply to show that external conditions impinge upon the choices made by key personnel. The environment presents decision-makers with both opportunities and constraints. New scientific and technological developments may provide opportunities for the introduction of far-reaching changes in productive activities. These, in turn, have their impact on organizational structure. Changes in the technology of warfare, for example, have had consider-able impact on government agencies such as the Ministry of Defence. The significance of new technology on the Post Office when it was run as a government department is equally clear. After the Second World War the introduction of new technology such as subscriber trunk dialling (STD) revealed deficiencies in organizational structure. More importantly, the history of this period reveals clearly how the impact of a changing environment is mediated by the power struggles and strategic choices of powerful participants within the organization and in other parts of its environment. The Post Office's response to technological development was heavily influenced by hostilities between groups who stood to gain or lose by change (notably the engineers and traffic officers) and by important Treasury decisions which singled the department out for unfavourable treatment and low priority within government investment programmes. So while 'a rapidly changing technological function such as telecommunications might entail an organic administrative structure, its implementation will be conditional on the intervening variable of human choice' (Pitt, 1980, p.178). The development of management technologies in fields such as personnel selection, training and budgeting also offers scope for organizational choice. Government departments have experienced considerable change in all these areas in recent years under the influence of new ideas. The impact of American experience with output budgeting has been particularly noticeable, as regards both the initial enthusiasm for it and the subsequent scepticism.

Changes in legal and political conditions are significant for all organizations, and government departments in particular. Again they offer both opportunities and constraints. New legislation enlarging the scope of ministers' powers will have an immediate impact on the department, providing it with scope for interpretation through statutory instruments. Political issues will affect the way that departmental tasks are performed. For example, conflict in the Cabinet over the handling of the steel strike in 1980 affected the role of the Department of Industry in the management of the steel corporation and of the Department of Employment in the process of arbitration. In order to counter political opposition to drillings in south-west Scotland by the Atomic Energy Authority to determine the suitability of the area for the long-term burial of nuclear waste, the Scottish Office limited the scope of the public inquiry into the planning application, thus excluding the wider issue of waste disposal. The use of administrative powers, as well as the formulation of new policy responds to political pressures.

Changing economic conditions may serve to constrain or liberate organizations. In times of growth manufacturing enterprise will respond to new markets. Government departments have shown they are capable of considerable growth in the use of resources during periods of economic expansion. It has even been argued that bureaucrats, financed by grants and thus not motivated by the need to show a profit, obtain satisfaction from enlarging the bureau's budget. Indeed, bureaux are expected to propose additional activities and higher levels of spending (Niskanen, 1973). However, economic change may equally act as a constraint. When there is a down-turn in the economy accompanied by high inflation, there will be pressure to cut expenditure. This may have a considerable impact on the structure and methods of management in government organizations. Processes for resource allocation in government departments (see chapter 5) have varied over the years in response to a changing economic environment. Institutional and analytical changes have fluctuated in the search for a more rational and synoptic approach to the choice of policy options. In general it seems that the further British government entered a period of financial constraint, the greater the pressures for the introduction of techniques for the more rational analysis of public policy, especially in its budgetary aspects (Wright, 1980).

The different parts of an organization may have to react to different external conditions. Lawrence and Lorsch (1967) raise the problem of different parts of a single organization responding to different features of the technological and economic environment so that these responses have to be integrated into a coherent approach to organizational objectives.

The immediate environment of an organization such as a government department is likely to consist of other organizations. A focal organization (that which is the main point of interest - a government department in our case) may be said to interact with its 'organization set'. Part of this set will be predominantly concerned with the inputs to be processed by the focal organization. In the case of a government department, the organizations in this sector of the environment will include parliament (providing authority and funds), the Cabinet (providing new policies, strategies and objectives) and pressure groups (bargaining with expertise, co-operation and other resources valued by the department). On the output side will be those organizations which the department hopes to change in some desired direction, such as nationalized industries (investment plans, pricing policies), private firms and corporations (industrial location or technological development, for example), and other governments at home and abroad (such as local authority housing plans or French meat imports).

The organization-set concept of the environment, however, should not be allowed to restrict our view of the government department's environment since often on the 'output' side this will consist of social groups rather than formal organizations, such as pensioners, the unemployed, low income groups, immigrants, farmers and so on. Such groups may, of course, be represented by formal organizations such as interest groups. These will often constitute the 'feedback' into the focal organization from those whose interests are affected by departmental decisions, actions and projects. It would be interesting to plot the networks of interactions among the organizations of which government departments are the focal points to see whether such networks correspond to particular configurations. It is likely that a range of configurations would be found. A dyadic relationship is likely between a spending department and the Treasury over budgetary control, for example. Most interdepartmental co-ordination is likely to take the form of a 'wheel' network, where a particular department interacts with others which do not in turn interact over any particular issue. But this is only conjecture.

It is not possible to establish with any degree of certainty the relative importance of the various economic, political, legal and technological features of the environment. Even more difficult to measure is the impact of culture on organizations, though it is generally accepted that the culture of society surrounding an organization is vitally important for the way in which it operates (Hall, 1974, pp.304-6). Of particular importance to the study of government departments is the idea that the influence of culture increases as the technology of operations become less routine and standardized. The activity of governing would seem particularly susceptible to cultural impact. Indeed, it is usually thought of as inseparable from a country's culture. Hence the emphasis which we place on norms and values which condition administrative behaviour, often resulting in conflicts and contradictions as government organizations try to respond to a changing political culture.

ENVIRONMENTAL INFLUENCES: VALUES AND INSTITUTIONS

One common thread runs through the many different perceptions of organizational environments generated by social scientists. That is the normative quality of the environment. It seems to us that the dominant feature of organizational environments is a set of

cultural, political, e   ich control and
legitimize the differe   life. Such values,
and the ways in which   re important
implications for the g   organizations and
to the behaviour of th   ed to meet those
goals. We give specifi attention to these matters in the appropriate chapters. In this chapter we wish to suggest that the most
illuminating way of studying the organizational environments of
government departments is to think of them as a system of values
operationalized through institutions. In this way we can refine
the commonplace conclusion that government departments operate
within a political setting and are accountable to political leadership.

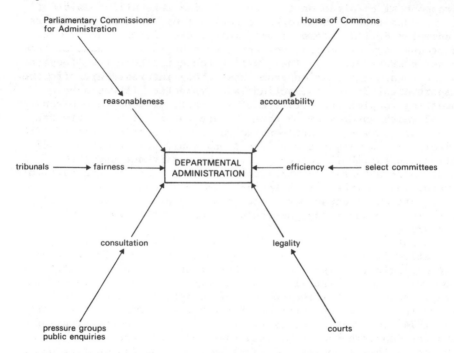

FIGURE 2.1   The environment of the government department

The values and institutions of the environment are set out in
diagrammatic form in Figure 2.1. The values identified (accountability, efficiency and so on) and the institutional arrangements
associated with them represent constraints imposed on departments
from the outside. These constraints are the expectations which the
community have about the way in which departments should operate.
Such expectations represent the dominant values of the community
which the departments 'serve'. The boundaries between these values,
and indeed between the departments and the institutions which make
up the environment, are not absolutely clear-cut. They do not
operate in watertight compartments. Any one part of the environment
may serve to enforce more than one set of values. Nor is the
'community' homogeneous. Different departments have different groups

of outsiders with which they come into close contact - clients or
claimants - to whom they defer in a wide variety of ways.
Nevertheless, values can be distinguished for analytical purposes to
show how they play an important part in setting the goals of
departments and delineating the methods by which those goals are
sought.

The values and institutions which constitute the environment of
central government departments in Britain are those of a broadly
liberal democratic political system. Some derive from rules and
conventions regarding the legitimate role of the administration, of
which central departments are the most important part, in a system
of representative and responsible government. Others, such as the
practice of consultation, are part of the political culture which
conditions the system of government as a whole. The political
consequences of these rules have hitherto received more attention
than their organizational consequences. Their implications for
the political institutions and processes themselves, such as
parliamentary sovereignty and ministerial responsibility, have
dominated the interest of social science in the political executive.
Our aim is to show how organizational life in government departments
is affected by the rules and pressures generated by the political
environment.

ACCOUNTABILITY

In February 1972 a report was presented to parliament by the Home
Secretary of a tribunal set up nearly a year earlier to inquire
into a number of issues relating to the cessation of trading by the
Vehicle and General Insurance Company. Among the conclusions of
the tribunal was that there had been negligence on the part of the
under-secretary who had been in charge of the insurance and companies
division of the Board of Trade from 1964 until the end of 1971 when
he had retired. Negligence was defined as a departure from the
required standard of competence judged in relation to the different
tasks and grades of different individuals. The tribunal decided
the under-secretary had been negligent because he did not display
initiative or imagination in considering the company's affairs
and because 'his performance as a whole fell so far below the
standard which could reasonably be expected from someone in his
position and with his experience (or opportunity to acquire
experience) ... we would call it incompetence'. He left his
subordinates to make decisions on suspect companies, rather than
consider them himself. He failed to lay down a sufficiently clear
and firm policy to prevent the company becoming complacent and his
department ineffective. And he did not possess the necessary
technical knowledge to be able to apply an independent judgment to
such cases. Two assistant secretaries in the same division were
also criticized, this time for a serious error of judgment,
insufficient firmness and over cautiousness. One's thinking was
said to have 'got into a groove'. 'His mind had become closed to
any approach or action which lay outside the policy line to which
he had devoted his efforts over a period of years'. The other was
said to have looked for reasons to justify inaction rather than
action.

So the officials were not only named, but also blamed. The
'responsible' ministers, however, were not found by the tribunal to
have been negligent. When the Prime Minister made his statement to
the House, one or two Members pointed out that the doctrine of
ministerial responsibility appeared to have been buried.

This case shows the gap between theory and practice which can
sometimes emerge in a principle fundamental to administration under
responsible government. The rule is that the political head of a
department of state should be answerable to the nation's elected
representatives for the actions and decisions of the officials who
serve him. Implicit in the doctrine is that the politician, not
the paid official, should receive the blame, praise (if any) or
censure in the event of administrative malfunctioning in the execution
of public policy as ultimately determined by parliament. There is,
of course, a great deal of controversy over how far such theoretical
principles actually operate at the political level. Our concern,
however, is not with such issues of contemporary political history,
but with the effects of the rules on the working lives of the staff
in government departments.

The first noticeable impact is reflected in the way work has to
be organized to deal with the political responsibilities of the
ministers who stand at the head of each department (see chapter 4).
Officials have to be very sensitive to the possibility of their
decisions causing political embarrassment to their minister. The
need for the department, through its minister, to defend its actions
in parliament, through Question Time, correspondence with Members
and participation in debates arising from statements, motions and
Bills, imposes a considerable administrative burden and has serious
implications for organizational structures. Departments together
have to deal daily with on average 160 questions from MPs requiring
oral or written replies. Not only answers but supplementary briefs
to support the minister in his confrontations with his critics
have to be supplied. This work requires senior members of staff
to spend a considerable amount of time collecting information from
the appropriate branches of the department. The routine and
planning activities of the department are frequently interrupted.
The administrative costs of accountability are high though difficult
to measure, as are the benefits.

All levels of the department work within the constraints imposed
by accountability. The knowledge that what the department does
must be publicly defensible, at least in terms of current policy,
leads to the adoption of certain bureaucratic features in the
organization, such as strict adherence to precisely formulated
procedures. We discuss the question of 'bureaucracy' in subsequent
chapters. This can, as we shall see, also lead to the bureau-
pathological traits of timidity, rigidity and delay in decision-
making. It can also set up conflicts between the demands of
accountability and the demands of efficiency which may judge
departmental performance by criteria requiring economy, speed and
risk-taking.

The whole ethos of work in departments is suffused with the
requirements of accountability. Officials are recruited in a way
which emphasizes their detachment from partisan politics. In order
that political praise and blame should (normally) be levelled only

against those who can be removed from office by democratic procedures, civil servants are recruited on the basis of merit demonstrated in open competitions, rather than by political patronage and favour. Constitutionally, civil servants are the permanent servants of the Crown, to be distinguished from the Crown's temporary servants, Her Majesty's ministers. Of course, in reality civil servants act as the servants of ministers and take decisions in their name. Their code of conduct requires allegiance to the state and, particularly at senior levels, abstention from political participation.

The work of the official in a government department is also characterized by anonymity. The official is protected individually from political criticism (though by no means collectively, as the interest of the public from time to time in salaries and other benefits shows). This applies particularly to senior officials whose opinions, advice and decisions are not open to public evaluation except in so far as they are regarded as the actions of ministers. Anonymity leads inevitably to confidentiality. Civil servants cannot afford to have their views and policy preferences known if they are to give loyal service to different ministers. And ministers have a vested interest in not revealing too many of the options which they have rejected. The freedom with which civil servants can give advice is believed to need protection by confidentiality.

However, the importance of anonymity and confidentiality varies from one level of the organizational hierarchy to another, and between administrative (generalist) staff and professionals (specialists). It is of far greater significance to senior officials working in Whitehall than to those in regional, district and local offices. There have also been cases when officials have been identified publicly as responsible for certain decisions, usually when something has gone badly wrong (as in the case of the Vehicle and General Tribunal). The giving of evidence in public to parliamentary committees is also found compatible with the constitutional position of civil servants. On rare occasions officials are identified by their ministers as being committed to a line of action unacceptable to the minister. The working life of the official in a government department, then, is influenced by a combination of constitutional doctrine and political expediency. Neither should be underestimated, as the vigorous attempt to enforce constitutional doctrine in the case of the late Richard Crossman's memoires shows. In that particular case, unlike the Vehicle and General affair, it was deemed politically necessary to invoke the convention by a government some of whose members were embarrassed by the revelations anticipated in the published diaries of an ex-Cabinet colleague. They sought through the doctrine to prevent publication.

EFFICIENCY

In its report of July 1974 on Public Expenditure on Transport the Environment sub-committee of the House of Commons Expenditure Committee expressed the belief that if a proper allocation of resources is to be achieved in -the transport sector, and transport

policy is to be co-ordinated, it is important that public investment
in road, rail and water transport is appraised on a comparable basis.
The Committee had taken evidence, both written and oral, from the
Treasury and the Department of the Environment, including the
latter's two principal finance officers, deputy director general of
highways, director of transport economics and chief statistician.

The officials claimed that comparability was achieved, even
though rail investments were analysed on a purely financial basis
and the major inter-urban road network on a cost-benefit ratio.
British Rail's policy of market pricing ensured that most benefits
to users are fully reflected in revenues and so internalized in the
rate of return.   The sub-committee, however, was not convinced,
doubting whether the full benefits of rail investment were in fact
reflected in the financial return.   Their view was that financial
criteria were not comparable with the criteria used to appraise
road investment.   They concluded that the department's general
approach to the evaluation of inter-urban transport investment
appeared ad hoc, confused and not conducive to the comparison of
road and rail investment on a consistent basis.   It could lead to a
misallocation of resources.   They recommended that, in the interest
of transport co-ordination and a proper allocation of public
expenditure, canal, road and rail investments should be analysed
on a strictly comparable basis.   Such analysis might show that the
marginal return of one mode of transport was higher than another
after taking into account the subjective assessment of environmental
and economic factors.

In March 1975 the Department of the Environment published its
observations on the sub-committee's report.   The department repeated
its claim that, despite technical difficulties in achieving exact
comparability, the cost-benefit test and the financial test produced
answers as comparable as possible in view of the different
institutional frameworks of the different modes of transport.   Exact
comparability would only be possible if a common pricing or taxing
scheme could be introduced.   Cost-benefit appraisal could be added
to the evaluation of financial return for rail projects, but mainly
in urban transport services such as the London-Heathrow rail link,
the Great Northern suburban electrification scheme or the Victoria
Line.   The DoE would, however, continue in association with the
nationalized industries concerned, to develop the application of
sound and consistent investment criteria throughout the transport
field.

This exchange of views between a parliamentary select committee
and a government department shows that in addition to the pressures
for accountability there is a public expectation, channelled again
through parliamentary procedure, that government departments will
be efficient.   New techniques of planning and management have been
developed in departments in the course of a continuous dialogue
with the House of Commons.   Originating in a concern that public
money should only be spent on projects authorized by parliament,
and not misappropriated, parliamentary scrutiny has developed in
the direction of eliminating waste and extravagance, of encouraging
sound practices in budgeting, contracts and financial administration
generally, and of obtaining value for money.   Departments are now
required to budget on a five-year forward projection and to present

public expenditure proposals more systematically and comprehensively
(see chapter 5).

Every area of departmental policy-making is now potentially
subject to parliamentary scrutiny by select committees with very
broad terms of reference. Again there are administrative costs to
be borne as departments organize themselves to justify their policies
and policy-making. The knowledge that their accounts will be subject
to audit acts as a deterrent against negligence, fraud, overspending
and illegality. Policies are reappraised as departments are
motivated by parliamentary scrutiny to think again. Developments
in financial planning, management techniques and structures, and
policy reviews have been influenced by select committees. The
introduction of output budgeting, management by objectives and
techniques of project appraisal such as cost-benefit analysis are
departmental responses to the demand for efficient administration
generated by the organizational environment.

LEGALITY

Upon discovering, early in 1975, that the price of a television
licence was to be increased on 1 April, a large number of people
bought new licences at the old rate before their existing licences
had expired, thus saving themselves about £6 each. About 36,000
people could have benefited from this. However, the Home Secretary
attempted to avoid this loss of revenue by threatening that unless
the extra six pounds were paid, licences would be revoked under
section 1(4) of the Wireless and Telegraphy Act of 1949. The Home
Office argued that if new licences were issued to persons already
holding licences due to expire after 31 March the savings to the
licence holders could amount to as much as £6½ million. The 1949
Act, it was argued, imposed no obligation to grant a licence to
cover a period for which a licence is already held. And it would
be neither fair nor sensible for someone who already has permission
to use a receiver to be given it a second time.

One licence-holder appealed and the court held that the minister's
action was unfair, unjust and unlawful. It constituted an improper
exercise of discretionary power as a means of levying money which
the executive had no authority to demand. Although the Home
Secretary had an undoubted discretion under the Act to revoke a
licence, that discretion was fettered to the extent that the courts
would intervene if it was exercised arbitrarily or improperly. In
this case the court decided it could and should intervene to declare
the proposed revocation unlawful, invalid and of no effect. In
the course of his submissions counsel for the Home Office said that
if the court interfered it would not be long before its powers
were called in question. The judge replied that the court trusted
this was not said seriously, but rather as a piece of advocate's
licence.

A fundamental principle generated by the political environment
is that the decisions and actions of officials in government
departments should be within the law. A department must not be
'ultra vires', or beyond its powers. It must not exceed its
statutory responsibilities, it must do what it is statutorily obliged

to do, it must follow prescribed procedures (if any) and it must act
without negligence, unreasonableness, bad faith or ulterior motive.
The courts have enforced these qualities on administrative action
through judicial review at the instigation of aggrieved citizens.
This is not to say, however, that such defects are unlikely to be
found in the future. As government grows more complex and distrust
of the state increases, as it seems to for a wide range of political
reasons, administrative actions are bound to be challenged and tested
for legality in the courts. This is another fact of life for the
official whose work is tested against external criteria.

The values in operation here are sometimes referred to as the
Rule of Law. They have important consequences for administrative
action in government departments. Officials must be prepared to
justify the legality of their actions. This may mean that they
behave bureaucratically and consequently become subject to criticism
for not being humane, liberal-minded or sympathetic. Desmond Keeling,
a senior civil servant who has written about management in government
departments, describes administration as being distinguished by an
attitude of mind conditioned by a concern for legality. He
characterizes the administrative system in a department as 'quasi-
judicial' in terms of working procedures, structures and objectives.
The qualities of conformity and consistency are identified as of
particular importance.

> Legal concepts like equity, embracing such principles as the
> equality of all individuals before the law, natural justice and
> the right of the applicant to express his views before a decision
> is reached, must always be in the forefront of the minds of those
> working in administrative systems. (Keeling, 1972, p.95)

CONSULTATION

At the end of January 1976 the Prime Minister was asked in the House
of Commons to list all the Royal Commissions appointed during the
past twenty years, showing how much they had all cost. The list
contained twenty-two commissions, nine of which could not be costed
(generally because they had not yet finished their work). The
remaining thirteen cost £1,410,476. This is but the tip of the
iceberg when it comes to the formal advisory machinery which
surrounds the central departments of state.

It is now almost a convention of the constitution that government
departments should consult with interested parties and other affected
interests in the course of formulating their policies. A complex
pattern of formal and informal methods of seeking and channelling
information now constitutes part of the culture within which
departments work. Society, or rather sections of it, feels it has
a right to be consulted and the government has increasingly
acknowledged a duty to consult. This is all part of the growing
importance of functional representation in society and the exertion
of political pressure and influence through sectional and promotional
organizations. The power of pressure groups in British government
has been legitimized by the close consultative links between
departments of state and the leaders of important interests. Often
the right to be consulted is enshrined in statute, as in the case

of local authority associations in the determination of rate support grant and teachers' salaries.

The formal aspects of consultative relationships between departments and the outside world are represented by the large number of commissions, councils, committees and boards which at any one time surround the organizations of central government. This method of consultation is structured in a variety of ways. Some departments have permanent advisory bodies attached to them, such as the National Advisory Council on Training Magistrates, the Council for Scientific Policy and the National Economic Development Council. Others set them up to do a finite task. Examples here are Royal Commissions or departmental committees of inquiry. Most advisory bodies work with departments at the national level, but some are regional in scope, such as the economic planning councils and others are local, such as the national insurance advisory committees.

This source of information for departments consists of over 300 advisory bodies at the national level alone (the number varies from year to year). Their functions are either consultative (such as the NEDC), expert (such as the Central Health Services Council) or administrative (such as the University Grants Committee). Often these functions are combined. The composition of advisory bodies also varies. There are those with a mixture of officials (civil servants or ministers) and the representatives and spokesmen of interests. Others consist wholly of experts from outside the ranks of the staff of the department concerned. Others are wholly representative in their membership, such as the National Advisory Council on the Training and Supply of Teachers. Members are usually selected by the minister concerned who is not, of course, bound by their advice and recommendations. Sometimes terms of reference are drawn very broadly, sometimes they are very specific. Recommendations will be based on evidence from outside and internal discussion. Sometimes research is carried out on behalf of the committee. Sometimes advice is given in confidence, sometimes in public.

There are both administrative and political reasons why departments set up formal methods of consultation, which means that the work of parent departments can be affected in different ways by advisory bodies. It also means they can exert some control over their sources of information, advice and pressure which affect them. Advisory and consultative bodies provide departments with information and advice from both experts and laymen which is not available from their own officials. Departments are also able to take into account the views of affected interests and so assess the likely reactions to changes in policy and administration from the sections of the public most concerned.

Related to and sometimes indistinguishable from these administrative reasons for consultation are political objectives. A department may try to obtain a politically neutral endorsement from its immediate environment for something it wishes to do or has made up its mind to do. Or it may wish to postpone a decision on some difficult issue. It may try to 'capture', 'co-opt' or 'nobble' opponents and potential critics, or win the support of affected interests through their involvement in the decision making process. There may be political advantage in a public declaration that an impartial and independent investigation has taken place.

Critics can be pacified and given the impression that something is
being done when it is not, as in the case of the 1970 Advisory
Council on Noise Abatement. Advisory machinery may even be used to
kill a proposal. A department may try, through the appointment of
an advisory body, to create the illusion that it is being influenced
in some direction and so quieten criticism, as was the case with the
Council for Wales and Monmouthshire. Many advisory bodies serve
more than one political purpose in the course of their lives.

In performing these administrative and political functions many
different facets of departmental work are affected. At one extreme
there are fundamental changes in public policy eventually embodied
in new laws. At the other there are administrative recommendations
and policy advice to subordinate agencies (such as Department of
Education and Science circulars to local authorities).

Between the formal machinery of advisory bodies and the free for
all of lobbying and pressure group activity there has grown up since
1967 a practice of publishing consultative documents, for the
benefit of expert and interested opinion, before a minister has
decided on a line of policy. The publication of Green Papers,
discussion papers and consultative documents now frequently
precedes decisions by the government on whether or not to initiate
legislation in parliament. This trend started as part of a plan
for more open government and greater public participation, two
recent fashionable demands. Also reflected here is the feeling
that major interests ought to be consulted and that better decisions
are likely to result from consultation prior to the government
deciding on a plan of action. In so far as the departments which
invite consultation in this manner are listing genuine choices of
public policy, it is reasonable to assume that when decisions are
eventually taken they will have been influenced by outside
organizations or individuals. But it is notoriously difficult to
establish how far particular policy decisions are influenced by
particular agents through consultation.

Other forms of consultation have more dramatic results. In
June 1976 police had to be called in by an inspector from the
Department of the Environment after protestors and demonstrators
had broken up a public inquiry into proposals to build a nine-mile
length of the M25 London Outer Orbital Motorway from the north
end of the Dartford Tunnel at Grays, Essex, to Brentwood. The
protestors shouted down every attempt by the inspector to open the
inquiry. He was eventually forced to allow the leader of the
protestors to state why they thought the inquiry should not even
take place. When it later became impossible for the department's
counsel and engineer to make their statements, the police were
asked to evict the protestors. This performance was repeated on
the second day of the inquiry and within an hour of the inquiry
being reopened about a third of the objectors had been removed by
the police. Conservationists leading the protest maintained that
an earlier inquiry into the line of the motorway had not been held
properly and also that they had the right to counter official
claims that a motorway was needed at all. The DoE on the other
hand, maintained that general transport policy cannot be debated
at inquiries. That was the task of parliament. Debates on the
need for roads is thus out of order at public inquiries which are

seen by the department as being concerned purely with local issues, such as the route to be taken.

So another source of information, often difficult to handle, provided by the political environment is the public inquiry. As the activities of government departments have increased in the public interest, private interests have often felt threatened. The latter have been successful in establishing the principle that when major government projects seem likely to come into conflict with private rights, especially rights to private property, there should be formal mechanisms for private views and opinions to be expressed. Consequently, government departments include the holding of inquiries in their decision-making processes for a diverse range of matters. The most numerous are held in connection with land-use planning, as might be expected, but opportunities for objections to be raised have also been provided by government departments concerned with road construction, the designation of national parks and new towns, local government reorganization, the setting up of rural development boards, police force reorganization, the regrouping of water undertakings and the reorganization of sewage disposal. The right to a hearing has become as ubiquitous as the right to be consulted.

It is now usually accepted that public inquiries are concerned with cases in which the private citizen is at issue with a public authority and involve the weighing of administrative proposals against private interests. Because of the clash of interests and the weighing of evidence, judicial criteria have increasingly been applied to the holding of inquiries by departments. They are supposed to be open, fair and impartial. The departments which hold inquiries tend to regard the minister's inspector or representative as his 'eyes and ears' and as such contributing to the flow of information into the department on the basis of which decisions are taken. But the judicial view of inquiries now seems to be accepted and the language of legal proceedings is frequently used in connection with the 'evidence' given, the presence of 'interested parties', the 'cross examination' of witnesses, and references to the inspector as 'judge'. Departments are now under an obligation to act fairly and reasonably when the facts of an inquiry are before them. It is also expected that the rules of natural justice will be observed at inquiry proceedings. All this has far-reaching consequences for the departments concerned, as do the misunderstandings and consequent frustrations frequently expressed by members of the public who become involved.

The departments have to organize their own inspectorates or appoint outsiders to hold their inquiries. The information produced is given a special status within the department. Administrative decision-making becomes more cautious and meticulous when it is evaluated by reference to the rights of individuals and the demands of natural justice. Once again the departments feel the conflicting pressures from the environment, in this case from a public or client group which wants both speedy decisions and the application of judicial principles to ensure fairness. All such factors have to be borne in mind whether the department is instigating a formal inquiry or dealing with an appeal through more orthodox administrative procedures.

FAIRNESS

Many departments administer functions which arise from the creation
of statutory rights. The law has come increasingly to specify
services, benefits and exemptions to which individual clients or
claimants are eligible provided they meet certain conditions. The
most frequent and obvious cases arise within the social security
field, but the same principles apply to direct taxation, property
valuation, import licences, industrial incentives, agricultural
grants and immigration control. What the responsible department
has to decide is whether a particular case falls within a category
to which certain rules apply. Discretion obviously has to be used
in many such cases. Decisions may consequently be challenged, not
on the grounds that they are illegal, but that the official has
reached an inappropriate decision given the circumstances of the
case as perceived by the applicant. Such conflicts between the
department and the citizen must be resolved in a way which is
accepted as fair by both sides. Consequently, some departments have
an adjudicatory stage tacked on to the end of the decision-making
process. Administrative tribunals have been set up to reconsider
the facts of a case, review the department's contended decision and,
if necessary, substitute a new decision for it.
    The decisions of tribunals feed back into the departments to
which they are attached. They provide precedents to guide subsequent
interpretations of the law and exercises of discretion. They place
a special responsibility on departmental officials to take reasoned
decisions which will stand up under scrutiny of a tribunal. Codes,
departmental rules, guidelines and instructions have to be
formulated to control the discretion of officials when working
within broad and perhaps vague statutory prescriptions. The
organizational hierarchy may have to be structured to regulate
discretion in a particular way. In the case of social security,
for example, regional and local managers control decision-making
to fit local circumstances to a certain extent. The existence of
an appeals procedure may bring informal aspects of organizational
behaviour into operation, such as a more liberal exercise of
discretion towards clients or claimants who threaten to use the
appeals machinery. Factors such as these have hitherto been
regarded by observers more from the point of view of the citizen,
the working of tribunals and abstract principles of rights and
justice, than from the perspective of organizational behaviour in
government departments, about which we still know relatively little.

REASONABLENESS

In 1975 the Parliamentary Commissioner for Administration (the
'Ombudsman') investigated a complaint about maladministration in
the Department of Health and Social Security. The department had
refused to backdate payment of a war widow's pension awarded in
1975. When her husband died in 1962, the widow applied for a war
widow's pension. This was rejected by DHSS on the grounds that
her husband's death had not been due to his wartime service. The
widow, however, claimed that deprivations suffered by her husband

when a prisoner of war in Java had in fact caused the illness from which he subsequently died. An appeal in 1964 to a Pensions Appeal Tribunal was rejected in support of the department's original decision. However, in 1972 fresh medical knowledge became available and the appeal was heard again in 1974. This time the tribunal decided in favour of the claimant.

The department eventually agreed to pay the pension as from 1970 but the claimant argued it should be backdated to 1962, the date of the original claim. The department's view was that they were simply following the rule embodied in their statutory instruments that pensions shall not be paid in respect of any period preceding the date of application or appeals as a result of which the claim for the award of pension is accepted.

Under the existing rules, then, there were no grounds on which the department could backdate the pension to the date of the husband's death. The Commissioner's view, however, after an investigation of the case, was that though there had been no maladministration, a rule which was normally sound had operated harshly and caused injustice, given the exceptional circumstances of this case. After reconsideration, the department eventually agreed to pay arrears of war widow's pension to 1962.

This case illustrates the kind of values which we have labelled 'reasonableness'. For this is yet another set of criteria by which departmental work is judged. To fall short of such standards is to be found guilty of maladministration. This concept has never been precisely defined, yet it has to be applied by the Parliamentary Commissioner to government departments when complaints falling within his jurisdiction are made about the quality of departmental decision making. Maladministration, aside from its grosser and therefore illegal forms such as bribery and corruption, is taken for practical purposes to mean defects in administrative procedures leading to hardship or injustice. Such defects as carelessness, inefficiency, incompetence, delay, ineptitude and arbitrariness constitute forms of maladministration.

There is, then, a distinction between the values implicit in the charge of maladministration and those which society and the political system attempt to enforce through parliament, the courts, administrative consultation and tribunals. Maladministration occurs when defects in official conduct or administrative procedures cause hardship or injustice when applied to individual cases. The relevant decisions are clearly not illegal, but their distinction from unfair exercises of discretion is not so clear. It is conventional to distinguish between appeals against a decision and complaints against the way a decision was reached. Maladministration is reserved for the quality of administrative procedures prior to the taking of a final decision rather than to the merits of a decision taken by the exercise of discretionary authority. However, even this distinction is blurred since cases have arisen in which, despite impeccable administrative procedures, a decision has resulted in manifest hardship to the complainant. The distinction between the quality of administrative procedures and behaviour and of decisions is sometimes difficult to draw. This becomes a question of identifying an unreasonable use of discretionary authority, of saying that a decision is one that no reasonable person could have taken. What is reasonable is not always self-evident, given the complexity of departmental objectives and statutory powers.

A similar problem occurs in the case of bad rules, where the proper administration of a departmental rule produces a harsh effect in some specific application of it. The operation of internal rules which departments draw up to control decision making are subject to parliamentary scrutiny via the Parliamentary Commissioner for Administration if they appear to cause hardship in their application. Departments may be required to review their rules if some hardship has been sustained.

Review of decision-making by an external agency testing for maladministration incurs costs for departments both in the investigation of the original case and in subsequent internal follow-ups which may be necessary if working procedures have to be adjusted. Such scrutiny may also induce caution (and, thereby, further allegations of delay). Low-level officials may be reluctant to exercise discretion for fear of the consequences and so push decision-taking up the hierarchy. Minor policy changes may have to be introduced, such as for the payment of tax arrears or the backdating of social security benefit. The Home Office has liberalized its rules regarding the access of prisoners to legal advice. Some changes have been quite trivial - such as changing the heading printed on official stationery used by Official Receivers so as to avoid giving the impression that they are acting on behalf of the Department of Trade. This probably means that the main effect of this part of the departmental environment is comparable to the rest in that it has the function of instilling in officials attitudes more conducive to the private interests of the public.

INFLUENCING THE ENVIRONMENT

The foregoing analysis may suggest that the government department is passively responsive to its environment. However, organizations can affect the environment in which they operate. This is as true of government departments as of any other formal organization.

In the first and most obvious place, departmental officials are not the passive instruments of ministerial leadership, party programmes and parliamentary enactment that constitutional doctrine would have us believe. We have already referred to the power of civil servants as a reason for subjecting government departments to systematic analysis. It is worth reminding ourselves how they can manipulate the environment in which they work. They may be able to influence ministerial choices, and thus the tasks which the department is called on to perform, in a variety of ways. They can control the information available to ministers. They can call on the support of colleagues in other ministries to use their influence with their ministers to bring pressure to bear at Cabinet level on a minister who wishes to go against the advice of his senior officials. They may be able to influence important elements of the central bureaucracy outside the departmental hierarchies, such as the Central Policy Review Staff, to support their

preferences against those of their ministers. By moving decisions
to interdepartmental levels, senior civil servants can win the
support of other departments in their conflicts with their ministers.
Mr Tony Benn has described how he was deliberately misled, as
Secretary of State for Energy, by officials defending accepted
Whitehall attitudes on a series of nuclear accidents in the Soviet
Union, the United States and at Windscale; and on the choice between
the American pressurized water reactor and Britain's own design.
He also described how the CPRS allies itself with civil service
opinion and engages in 'organized subversion' by 'feeding' a
department's view which a minister is trying to block into other
parts of the Whitehall machine, especially Cabinet and Cabinet
Committees ('Guardian', 8 January 1980).

Then there is the discretion which has to be exercised in the
name of the minister in many areas of public policy. Here it is
important to distinguish between an exercise of discretion which
affects the way policy is implemented and one which, as a consequence
of policy implementation, brings about a change in the environment
which then feeds back into the department as part of the inputs
into the policy-making process. In one sense anything the
bureaucrat does affects the environment. An effective decision
may simply produce the change desired by policy-makers – a
reduction in the level of local authority spending, say. The
environment has been affected as intended. There may be unintended
consequences, though. Some of the immigration service's practices
when scrutinizing the claims of immigrants for entry permits have
caused public outcries. Here, then, is an unintended impact on
the environment which will undoubtedly feed back into the
procedures and operations of the Home Office. Finally, officials
may, through their discretionary powers, intentionally manipulate
the environment by influencing the expectations which people have
of the bureaucracy and thereby the claims which they make on it.
Hill has shown how discretionary payments under the social security
laws may come to be regarded as 'rights' so that any refusal of
such a payment can be regarded as a denial of 'rights': 'widespread
exercise of discretion in a particular way creates a presumption
that a deliberate policy exists and that such decisions are to be
expected in future' (Hill, 1972, p.71).

We have seen that part of the environment of government
departments, and a most important part, consists of the organized
interests and pressure groups which maintain more or less close
consultative links with the central bureaucracy. Here again, the
departments do not merely respond to pressure. They are capable
of orchestrating it. They can select the groups that they will
listen to. Access can be made easier for some than others. Groups
may be helped in their campaigns with vital information. For
example, in 1978 it was revealed that Department of Transport
officials had written memoranda arguing for a public inquiry into
'juggernaut' lorries in order to help the road haulage industry's
case. The inquiry was to be used as a way of dealing with political
opposition to heavier lorries. Departments also ally themselves
with groups to defend their own interests. In the case of the
Water Act of 1973 the Ministry of Agriculture's interests were
threatened when the Department of the Environment proposed to set

up Regional Water Authorities. MAFF was opposed to the loss of its control over land drainage to the DoE and its proposed RWAs. MAFF held meetings with its client groups, particularly the National Farmers' Union and the Country Landowners' Association, 'to plan a campaign to prevent the take-over' (Richardson and Jordan, 1979, p.56). The department organized the groups into putting 'pressure' on it to be used in its negotiations with DoE. Some departments see it as their job to promote interests with which they are involved. A former deputy secretary of the Department of Education and Science said that one of its jobs was to promote the cause of education. The department spends a great deal of time preparing briefs for the minister's public relations exercise on behalf of this political function. In some exceptional cases, such as the National Farmers' Union and the Ministry of Agriculture, Fisheries and Food, the closeness of collaboration amounts to virtually joint administration of agricultural policy.

The whole atmosphere within which departments are evaluated, whether by the public or parliament, is affected by the information available to outsiders. This the departments can control fairly effectively. The secrecy surrounding central administration makes it difficult for the public to obtain a clear understanding of the power relationships in Whitehall. Parliament has strengthened its capacity to scrutinize the administration, but even its most august committee finds it difficult to reveal the truth for the purpose of financial accountability. Recent cases suggest that the Public Accounts Committee, on which parliament increasingly depends for any effective scrutiny of public expenditure, experiences considerable difficulty in extracting the truth from government departments. A close analysis by one particular civil servant, attempting to wage a war on bureaucratic waste, of a case with which he was closely involved led him to conclude that the PAC's examinations are superficial and ineffectual. Many of the problems here arise from the nature of the task and the constitution of the committee, but they are exacerbated by the ease with which civil servants can conceal what they do not wish to reveal (Chapman, 1979).

One important feature of the organizational environment is legitimacy. 'It is generally assumed that an organization has a protected status in society as long as its output is considered legitimate' (Perrow, 1970, p.97). Legitimacy is dependent on the attitudes towards the organization of significant parts of the environment. If the organization and its products are consistent with significant values outside it its stability is helped. When those values change, organizational change is likely to follow. We see this most clearly in the constant fusion and fission of government departments as policy objectives are modified by a succession of ministers and governments.

Organizations inevitably attempt to control the level of legitimacy. 'One way to insure legitimacy is to bring into the organization those groups who would threaten its stability - a process called "co-optation"' (Perrow, 1970, p.97). We have already seen how government departments employ a large network of advisory committees drawing on the services of influential outsiders. As well as being 'an important channel of access for groups'

(Richardson and Jordan, 1979, pp.72-3) they provide the departments with important opportunities to influence outside thinking about the work of the department, to inform outsiders of departmental problems and views and to create a feeling of commitment to the department by the close association of significant members of external interests with its work.

Departments have also spawned a vast number of subordinate agencies to which a multitude of functions, so diverse as to be almost impossible to classify, have been delegated. Many such agencies have appointed boards of management on which outsiders serve. The parent department thus has an important power of patronage which again enables it to co-opt into administration interests which might otherwise be hostile to it. And there is, of course, something of a flow in the other direction, with civil servants moving out of Whitehall either temporarily or permanently. Temporary secondments are officially designed to develop more effective communication and understanding between government, business and other sectors. Permanent transfers, particularly after retirement, are more significant and raise questions about the possibility of unfair advantage to the new employer or of officials bestowing favours in the hope of future rewards. There also seems to be a practice developing of civil servants resigning to join pressure groups which have working relationships with their old departments. Thus the environment is to some extent determined by an outward flow of officials accompanying the co-option of outsiders and the 'colonisation of the private sector by government' mentioned earlier (Richardson and Jordan, 1979, pp.61-70).

Chapter 3

GOALS AND THE GOVERNMENT DEPARTMENT

It is a, by now, commonplace assumption in organizational analysis to direct attention to the fact that a distinguishing feature of organizations is their purposiveness and directedness in the attainment of objectives. Search of the literature on organizations quickly reveals that efforts have been made by many writers to categorize and define them as goal-seeking artifacts. Talcott Parsons (1960) captures the essence of this view by insisting that organizations are a species of social system 'deliberately constructed and reconstructed to seek specific goals or values', while Amitai Etzioni (1964) argues that organizations are systems of power, communication and responsibility deliberately planned with the intention of realizing specific goals. Both seek to differentiate organizations from other types of collectivity, such as social classes, families, work-groups, etc. While the demarcation sought by these writers is a relative rather than an absolute one (to a degree, classes, families, and work-groups may manifest rational planning and a consciousness of social objective), the intention is to suggest that organizations demonstrate purposiveness commonly in excess of that shown by other social institutions.

There is, then, widespread agreement among contemporary organizational analysts that organizations seek to reach specific targets or goals. Indeed we may go so far as to suggest that some writers see goals and goal-seeking behaviour as the key defining characteristic of organizations. On this view, it is logically impossible to call something an organization which does not pursue goals as part of deliberate policy. Perrow (1970, p.133) suggests 'a definition of goals is necessary and unavoidable in organizational analysis. Organizations are established to do something; they perform work directed toward some end. We must examine the end or goal if we are to analyze organizational behaviour'.

It is accepted here that this perspective must be adopted in examination of the organization in which we are interested. However, to talk of the goal of an organization may be misleading for several reasons. First, large complex organizations of the type with which we are presently concerned will, typically, have a variety of goals or ends to which the organization is striving. Some government departments, for example, may comprise a heterogeneous collection

of functions which are only loosely related and which provide them
with multiple purposes. In 1970, for example, following a White
Paper on the reorganization of central government, 'giant' departments
were established in Whitehall to co-ordinate activities which
previously had been located in many smaller departmental units. The
resulting conglomerate units, superficially simple in design and
conception, are extremely complex in structure and internal working.
Understanding such complexity will be a necessary part of any goal
analysis of contemporary government organization.

Second, it is widely recognized that useful as the concept of
goal may be, it can lead the analyst of organization to invest it
with dubious properties. Obvious problems await the uninitiated
determined to attribute the activities of individuals within the
organization to the organization itself. The danger here lies in
using the concept of the individual human personality as a
descriptive metaphor for the organization. Thus organizations
pursuing goals are described as acting, thinking and making decisions.
Pitfalls can arise from such analysis. In particular the assumption
may creep in that the organization always acts through consensus
and agreement. The view may readily develop that singularity of
purpose will characterize organizational decision-making. The
problem here is admittedly complex and has not been satisfactorily
resolved in organizational analysis. The question remains to be
answered: to what extent are we justified in treating the
organization as a thinking, acting individual? The emergent
properties of organization are sufficiently important to suggest
that, in many important respects, departments are greater than the
sum of the individuals within them. They may be said to exist
independently of particular individuals and groups who staff them.
On this view they may be seen to function regardless of the fact
that individuals constantly join and leave them. Organizations
clearly outlive their inhabitants. It must not be forgotten,
however, that organizational members are important and may imbue
the organization with specific characteristics and traits.
Organizational analysis cannot escape paradox. Organizations
persist in spite of and because of the individuals within them.
There is inherent tension within any organization between its grand
structural design and the inhabitants; organizational analysis must
be sensitive to this level of analysis problem.

The first view of organizations, described above, namely that
they are greater than the sum of their individual parts, makes
obvious sense. There seems to be good reason for suggesting that
statements such as 'the Board of Trade acted' or 'the Treasury
view is' are sensitive to the common understanding that organizations
are identified in terms of a common purpose. There is a widespread
feeling that, in dealing with large bureaucratic organizations, the
individual is up against an impersonal machine staffed by automata
who merely carry out orders in deference to some higher command
which is assumed to exist but whose whereabouts are concealed.
This pessimistic view of large organizations is particularly
relevant to analysis of popular preconceptions and misconceptions
about the government department. Literature and films are replete
with examples of 'little men' dealing with large organizations:
sometimes, as in the writing of Franz Kafka, the hero is never able

to perceive the identify of his official tormentors who may, without redress, demand his allegiance, life and soul in the name of the organization. In addition, a 'stripping' or depersonalizing process of organizational socialization may be used in an effort to prise loose the individuality of new members and to blend their personality with that of the organization. Initiation rites, uniforms, official insistence on procedures - all are attempts to indoctrinate the individual in the view that he must link his fate to the corporate existence, although it is only in the most doctrinaire organization that the depersonalization process is complete.

While acknowledging that this view is fairly common, we declare a preference for a 'pluralistic' view of organizations which accepts the fact that they are composed of relatively autonomous individuals and groups with widely varying notions about goals. While due attention must be paid to the view of organizations as entities having commonality of purpose (co-operative systems), we must also conceive of them as systems in which debate, dispute and conflict may arise over the ends to be pursued. Not only will there be multiple goals within large, complex organizations, but internal conflicts and those arising from the relationships binding the organization to its environment will affect its goal-seeking activities. Such conflicts over the ends to be pursued are a common feature of organizational life. Government departments as well as private sector organizations may be expected to manifest such conflict.

GOAL CLASSIFICATION

Considerable effort is devoted within the organization theory literature to a classification of goals. First, a distinction is drawn between formal and informal goals. Formal goals may be discovered by inspection of the organization's charter. In the case of a private company the obvious place to look for a formal statement of purpose is its articles of association. These may be expected to reveal the broad outlines of organizational goals. In the case of the government department we might look to the statutes empowering ministers to act in certain ways. We might also expect to find information in a wider variety of sources. In the 1970 White Paper on central government for example it was proposed to establish a Department of Trade and Industry whose duty would be 'to assist British industry and commerce to improve their economic and technological strength and competitiveness'. The problem with such statements, however, is that they are vague. To suggest that the Department of Trade and Industry would have the duty of assisting the development of British industry is no cast iron guarantee that in practice such an aim or goal will be achieved or, importantly, how that aim will be achieved. Both depend upon the activities of civil servants within the department. Unlikely as it may seem, civil servants might subvert this goal. We shall see that the power of key groups of civil servants is significant and may lead them to frustrate organizational objectives with which they fundamentally disagree. To discover whether the formal goal of the organization is pursued by its members it would be necessary to observe them in action and ask questions about their values. The problem with formal statements about organizational purpose is that they take no account of behavioural modifications to those goals which, in practice, may arise from processes of social interaction within and outside the organization.

Organizational theorists long ago discovered the importance of informal organization - unscheduled processes of social interaction and individual behaviour - which may or may not work to foster the attainment of formal, stated ends. A fascinating dilemma arises in any organization from the fact that, while the informal processes within it may frustrate the attainment of formal objectives, the organization apparently requires the informal component to enable it to function effectively. In the case of the large bureaucratic organization some studies have indicated that its informal structures are essential for ensuring responsiveness to changes in its task and environment. A broad-based analysis must take into account the social relationships which develop within the organization. Examination of such relationships will reveal that behaviour is not inevitably aimed at attaining formal, i.e. stipulated, goals. On the contrary, study of the informal organization will reveal some work practices congruent with the attainment of the formal objectives, while others will be shown to cause deviations from them. Informal goals will emerge in the context of daily routine supporting a range of activity sometimes bearing tenuous relationship to formal goals. We heard recently of a civil servant who had deliberately taken a job with the Department of the Environment because it enabled him to plan a trip by Land Rover to Australia. Similarly, the much publicized trial of the architect John Poulson and permanent secretary George Pottinger is eloquent testimony to the ability of civil servants like members of other organizations to pursue their own self interest even when it brings them into conflict with formal goals.

Another important distinction is made in the literature between formal and real goals. Use of the terms 'formal' and 'real' sensitizes us to look for divergence between what organizational members say they are doing and what they are actually doing. We may spot the difference between the formal and the real by examining the resources, measured in terms of time, effort and materials spent in attaining a set of objectives. If no resources are devoted to formal goals while considerable energy goes into non-scheduled activities and goals we may say that the formal goal is dormant while the non-scheduled goal is active. Real goals then, are goals which the organization actively pursues. They may be consistent with the formal goal or may supplement or displace it. We may ask why the formal goal remains in existence in the absence of any activity directly related to it. The answer lies in the legitimating function of the formal goal. An organization which can use a formal charter, for example, to underwrite its activities and convey the impression that it has a defined purpose worth pursuing may shield itself from hostile groups and individuals in its environment.

We are daily confronted with the actions of organizations, including government departments, whose ostensible aims sometimes appear to diverge from their real aims. A recent example is the case of the American journalists Hosenball and Agee. Acting in his role as guardian of state security, the Home Secretary instituted deportation proceedings against them for supposed infringements of the Official Secrets Act. Both were accused of publishing books and articles contrary to the security interests of Britain. Their case caused considerable public protest. Many felt that they had not been found in breach of British state security, but that the Home Secretary was using this charge as a subterfuge for obliging the US State Department in Washington. The American government wanted deportation proceedings to be successfully concluded. The journalists were alleged to have reduced the effectiveness of the Central Intelligence Agency by their reports on its activities. Deportation proceedings are secret so it will be some time before we can discover whether the Home Secretary was pursuing the formal goal of British security or the real goal of diplomacy.

Finally, we draw attention to an important distinction between the output goals of the organization and its system goals. Output or end product goals refer to what the organization actually produces. In the case of a government department we can look to the services it provides for the community, for example social welfare benefits or decisions relating to land-use planning. In contrast, system goals refer to the internal state of the organization, the methods and working practices which have been adopted to accomplish output objectives. The relationship between the system goals and the output goals is a relationship between means and ends. Ends or outputs must be related to means or inputs (resources), in such a way that efficient and effective organization may result. For any given output there is likely to be a choice of inputs. If the choice of ends is problematical, the choice of the correct or appropriate means to achieve them will also cause concern. In government an example of a system goal is the procedure adopted by the DHSS for ensuring the fair and impartial assessment of claims for welfare benefits.

GOAL DISPLACEMENT

It was the German sociologist Robert Michels (1915) who argued that attention must be given to the process whereby the goals of organizations are displaced by groups within them. Such groups may redefine the purposes of organizations, so diverting them from their paths. The phenomenon of goal displacement has been employed in the analysis of business organizations and trade unions by later writers and can be employed to good effect in the analysis of government departments.

Departments are bureaucratic organizations. That is to say, they have a well defined system of rules and structure of authority. There is a highly developed division of labour within them. They employ a hierarchical chain of command. Promotion and appointment are attained on the basis of achieved attributes or seniority. The bureaucratic organizational form is, arguably, one of the greatest achievements of contemporary culture. Bureaucracy as a set of organizational principles has been found essential for the production of the goods and services demanded by modern civilization. This is why it is a dominant issue in all branches of organizational analysis and one which will reappear at various stages in this book. Max Weber first charted its ascendancy as the prime form of social organization in industrial society.   But if bureaucracy brings undoubted benefits, considerable effort and ingenuity have been expended by sociological writers to demonstrate that it has seemingly inescapable weaknesses. We shall see in chapter 5 that improvements in the bureaucratic form of organization in central government have often been sought. Here we note that goal displacement is widely seen as an inevitable consequence of the bureaucratic form.

The inherent paradox of the bureaucratic form, of which the government department is a good example, is that the very rules which enable it to function as an effective administrative instrument may, under certain circumstances, thwart its goal-seeking activities. The rules of the organization may prevent, rather than encourage, the attainment of organizational objectives. The individual bureaucrat may become so engrossed in the rules and regulations governing administration in his department that he loses sight of the ends which the organization formally exists to serve. Instrumental values become terminal values. This leads to a rigid application of rules regardless of whether or not they have outlived their usefulness in a changing situation. Various forces operate on the individual to induce caution. The existence of rules protects the individual bureaucrat. If he can demonstrate that he is acting within permissible limits he can effectively forestall the criticisms of his superiors. Timidity and caution are widely perceived characteristics of government bureaucracies, though the British civil service is not alone in being subjected to criticism over the years for its bureaucratic failings. As we shall see, the structure of British central government and the operating conventions affecting its working, tend to encourage members of departments to be hesitant and cautious. They are anxious to avoid political embarrassment for ministers. Such an environment may lead to a form of goal displacement. The upward referral of decisions and resulting centralization may produce negative consequences in terms of goal-seeking activities. Over-conformity to rules leads departments to become set in their ways and unresponsive to change. The Fulton Report on the civil service in 1968 drew attention to this tendency (we shall argue below that it overstated the case against existing government department organization) and proposed alternative structures and strategies for inducing change in the organizations it considered.

A common complaint directed at government departments arising out of the rigid application of rules is that of 'red tape'. Literally, red tape is the tape used to bind together government papers. Hence the more red tape, the more papers. Many critics see red tape as an inevitable by-product of the bureaucratic organization. Red tape is not necessarily to be seen as a negative feature of bureaucracy. We should all become anxious if departments suddenly started behaving as if rules and precedents no longer mattered. We have seen in our examination of the environment of the department that institutionalized values play a part in prohibiting certain organizational acts and encouraging others. They provide limits to behaviour, prescribing what is

acceptable, and proscribing the unacceptable. They are an inevitable
feature of any large contemporary organization. Departments, in
common with other bureaucratic organizations, have both positive
and negative features. The problem of organizational management
is to maximize the one and minimize the other.

Two common criticisms are current with regard to the bureaucratic
organization. The first states that it is particularly unsuited to
conditions of change.   The second suggests that it is prone to rule-
following to the detriment of long-run considerations. The two are
closely and clearly linked. The first view sees bureaucratic
organizations as hidebound by precedent and staffed by individuals
whose behaviour is resistant to change. C. Northcote Parkinson in
a waspish book published some years ago documented the tendency for
work to increase in government offices 'to fill the time available'.
By an inevitable law of work proliferation, rules and papers would
increase ensuring the employment of greater and greater numbers of
individuals. Even if the actual importance of a government function
decreases, the number of public servants would increase and go on
increasing. Once in a post, people will resist any attempts to
cut down their power and render them redundant. They become
resistant to changes aimed at increasing overall efficiency.
Similarly, 'Gresham's Law' states that long-run considerations will
be sacrificed in the interests of day-to-day routine. Civil
servants will tend to abandon, or relegate to secondary importance,
matters which do not have immediate impact. Once again, the cause
of this is the conventional setting within which civil servants
work. In particular, the effect of ministerial responsibility to
parliament may lead the department to concentrate its energies on
averting criticism in the House of Commons.

GOAL SUCCESSION

The concept of goal displacement must be distinguished from the
concept of goal succession. Under the latter are subsumed those
cases in which the organization, having achieved its stipulated
purpose, is concerned to take up another cause in order to survive
and maintain its integrity. The world of organizations like the
world of nature may be said to abhor a vacuum. The most oft cited
example of goal succession is that documented by David Sills (1957).
Sills studied the Foundation for Infantile Paralysis in the United
States. Staffed by volunteers, it raised money to combat the
disease of polio and was highly successful in supporting medical
research which ultimately led to its virtual elimination. But
with this goal achieved, the organization did not go out of
existence. Instead, new goals were found which permitted its
members to continue offering voluntary service to the community, a
much prized activity.

Etzioni (1964) points out that true cases of goal succession
are rare because few organizations are as successful in attaining
their goals as the Foundation. In addition many organizations which
achieve the goals set for them by their founders do not go on to
aim for fresh goals. They are dissolved or disappear.

Departments frequently acquire new goals. In the twentieth

century British central government has broadened its activities
requiring the utilization of new skills. The state no longer merely
carries out the traditional 'nightwatchman' role of maintaining law
and order at home and in an imperial setting. Governments have
become increasingly involved in actively pursuing social and
economic goals. Two world wars resulted in a significant expansion
of state powers. Changes in the nature and extent of central
government activity have not occurred in an administrative vacuum.
The system of departments has had to respond to changes which have
taken place in its workload. The older departments, such as the
Treasury, Post Office, Home Office, Department of Education, and
Foreign Office have been supplemented during the twentieth century
by an array of departments to cope with the new activities. As new
functions develop, they may lead to the creation of separate
departments, or they may be fused on to an existing department.
Similarly, the increasing importance of a function carried out
within a multi-functional department may lead to its fission and
transfer elsewhere, maybe to a separate organization. Hanson and
Walles (1975) draw attention to the processes of 'creation, fission,
fusion and transfer' which have occurred in the development of the
constellation of departments which we know today. Such occurrences
have become increasingly important. For example, in 1964 the
incoming Labour government created a Department of Economic Affairs
to develop planning functions previously performed by the Treasury.
Similarly, in 1970, new 'giant' departments were established to
co-ordinate functions which had previously been separately organized
under a variety of different departments. The Departments of Trade
and Industry and of the Environment were established by the
Prime Minister Edward Heath to bring about a 'new style of
government'. Such creation may be linked to a process of fusion
or fission. Under the first, activities are grouped together under
one head for the purpose of administration. For example, the
Ministry of Health, newly created in 1918, fused together a series
of social and welfare functions previously administered separately.
Conversely, in 1974, the conglomerate functions of the Department
of Trade and Industry were separated out in an effort to reverse
the process of fusion begun in 1970. Lastly, the transfer of
functions between various departments has been fairly common,
depending on a variety of political and organizational pressures.
   As the tasks of government change, so the agencies through which
they are administered change. Such a shift in tasks shows that
goal succession is far more complex in government than in the special
case described by Sills. First, government activity is continuous.
Many of the goals of government cannot easily be accomplished on a
once-for-all basis. Very often there is no finite, clear-cut
solution to a problem. The task of providing welfare and defence
is never-ending - the poor and wars are always with us. Second,
new problems are perceived. After the Second World War the founders
of the National Health Service envisaged that the application of
increasing resources would prevent and cure the major diseases of our
age. While immense progress has been made in combatting diseases
such as tuberculosis, new ones have taken the place of the old with
ominous regularity. TB clinics have been superseded by intensive
care units for coronary illness. The importance of psychological

illness has been belatedly recognized. In short the diseases of
poverty have been replaced by the diseases of affluence. For a
rigorous definition of goal succession to apply it would be necessary
to demonstrate that the Ministry of Health had successfully overcome
disease and was now concentrating on other activities. In actual
fact quite the reverse is the case. This raises a third important
issue. While the activities of government may change, the overall
nature of basic government activity remains remarkably constant.
Goals are constantly modified as political leaders devise new
policies to deal with recurring problems. The work of government
may be viewed as being subject to a constant process of goal
modification under the influence of party politics. Ideological
differences lead to constant shifts in public policy. New goals
arise as changing values are applied to recurring problems. For
example, the management of the economy has been subjected to both
Keynesian and monetarist economic philosophies.

   Thus in government goal succession involves not only the
acquisition of new tasks (for example, energy conservation), but
also the redefinition of old tasks (for example, Britain's changing
military role) and the persistence of existing problems for which
solutions are not found (for example, unemployment).

GOALS AND THE POLICY-MAKING PROCESS

A longstanding fiction of the British constitution is that
politicians decide and the civil servants or bureaucrats execute
those decisions. Such a view of the government department downgrades its central importance in the policy-formulating process.
A view of the department as passively putting into effect decisions
made by the political executive (Cabinet) provides, in effect, an
extremely naive view of the role of the civil servant in the
political process in Britain. It assumes a coincidence between
the formal goal of the department and the actual or real goal.
Legalistic or constitutional views of the department as we suggested
in chapter 1 tend to see it in transmission belt terms. This is a
mistaken way of viewing a key locus of decision-making activity in
the British system of government.

   In fact, many writers have recognized that the real goals of the
government department have involved it directly not only in the
policy-executing process but also in the policy-making process.
As early as the 1860s, the English philosopher John Stuart Mill
felt able to claim that the system of government in this country
involved the bureaucracy directly not only in the rule-application
(administrative) process in society but also in the rule-making
(political) process. Mill recognized the potential power of the
bureaucratic official and was anxious about its consequences. The
more the bureaucracy involved itself in the political process in
society the more cause for worry there should be; 'where everything
is done through the bureaucracy, nothing to which the bureaucracy
is averse can be done at all'. Here Mill expressed anxiety about
a problem which has concerned many modern writers on government;
the place of the non-elected official in the system of representative
government in a democracy. Max Weber also expressed concern about

the place of the bureaucratic government department in a democratic
system of government. Both Mill and Weber recognized the essentially
paradoxical nature of the permanent official. Called into existence
by the needs of government in a large-scale democratic society, he
assumes a dominant position in the political decision-making system.
Such a position could lead him to usurp the power of elected
governments. Under certain circumstances, bureaucracy - formally
the servant of democracy - might acquire a power position independent
of its political masters.

The increase in the scope and domain of government power in
Britain has created greater bureaucratic independence. By 1929,
Lord Hewart proclaimed that a 'New Despotism' had arrived (1929).
The power of the paid official was held to have increased to a point
at which he could no longer be held in check by parliament. Owing
to pressure of time and business, parliament had been forced to
delegate many of its legislative powers to ministers, which in
practice meant an increase in the power of the civil service. Hewart
saw in such a development the possibility of the civil service
exercising its power in a capricious and potentially dictatorial
manner.

We need not go as far as Hewart to agree that no model of the
political system which sees departments as passive executors of
policy will adequately represent the highly complex and interactive
nature of the policy-making process. An analysis of departments
as goal-directed must be based on a view of them as partially
autonomous decision-making systems. Brown and Steel (1979) suggest
that the most characteristic activity of a government department
is reaching decisions. This distinctly modern conception of
departments sees them as key initiators of policy decisions. On
this view, they do not simply wait to be told what to do by a group
of politicians; they are active in the process of deciding what
is to be done. The importance of this lies in the fact that it
dissolves a distinction commonly found in legalistic treatments
of British government, the distinction between politics and
administration.

According to old-style constitutional views of the department,
political decisions and administrative acts are separate activities.
Politics, on this view, is seen as the prerogative of the elected
politician and is concerned with the 'allocation of values' in
society. It establishes priorities or ends for society. In a
democracy the fiction is maintained that the elected politician
has a right to take strategic political decisions, leaving the
civil servant and the government department to provide the means
for putting those decisions into effect. The civil servant merely
devises the administrative apparatus for carrying out the policies
of the politician. Such a view suggests that it is possible to
separate out the political function in a democratic society and the
administrative function. An organizational view of departments
provides an alternative formulation. It suggests that the
political and the administrative functions of government are
inextricably linked and that the individual civil servant has a
key part to play in policy-choice as well as policy-implementation.

MINISTERS AND CIVIL SERVANTS

Understanding the relationship between the minister and the civil
servants in his department is crucial to an understanding of the
active role played by the department in the policy making process.
The civil servant can exercise considerable power in terms of certain
ministerial relationships. Concern has been expressed by politicians
and non-politicians alike over the accumulation of influence and
power at the top of the civil service. For example, Mrs Marcia
Williams, the personal and political secretary to Harold Wilson,
argued (1972) that the Labour governments of 1964-70 had to fight
a constant battle with civil servants in their efforts to fulfil
the election pledges which they had made. She presents a picture
of radical reforming governments faced with a civil service philosophy
of gradualism. She implies that civil servants are well placed to
thwart the aspirations of politicians and prevent them putting into
practice policies with which they, the civil servants, disagree.
On Mrs Williams' arguments, the civil service often acts 'as if it
is a sovereign power responsible only to itself'. The picture
painted of the top civil service in this account is one of
conservatism, social exclusiveness and power. A Labour government
seems particularly susceptible to negative influence from the
service. Mrs Barbara Castle, one time Secretary of State for
Employment and Minister of Transport has argued that, paradoxically,
the dange which the British civil service poses for democracy lies
in its excellence: it is a state within a state. She stresses the
relatively weak position that the minister is in when he assumes
office. He does not possess the knowledge to challenge effectively
views of officials in his department. Similar points have been made
by other ex-ministers and must be treated as serious comments on the
working of the political/administrative system. Most would accept
that it is necessary to strengthen the hand of the politician and
suggest that political counterweights to civil service supremacy
should be introduced such as the appointment of a 'ministerial
cabinet' of advisors providing an alternative source of ideas.
Such schemes, it is claimed, would help to reduce the dependence
of the minister on advice from civil servants who have a particular
view of an area of policy and administration.
  Recent political biographies and the variously reported
reminiscences of ex-ministers and civil servants leave an indelible
impression of the central place of the official in the decision-
making process of government. Richard Crossman, former minister
of Housing and Local Government, suggested that civil servants
virtually take over a minister's whole existence, body and mind.
The key official, the permanent secretary, dominates the whole
proceedings of the department and guides the minister towards
decisions which the civil service favour. If the civil service is
as impressively powerful as some of the above accounts would seem
to indicate we must ask what are the bases for such power.

CIVIL SERVICE POWER

The conventional view of power in the British system of government

precisely mirrors the view of organizations propounded by early
theorists. The man at the top (politician or entrepreneur) makes
decisions and issues orders to the machine which it promptly carries
out. Such a view of organization obfuscates more than illuminates.
It overlooks the fact that members of organizations have considerable
power resources enabling them to act in a highly independent and
'political' way. We have long conceived of the civil servant as
existing to offer advice to ministers - to 'encourage, warn and be
consulted'. But such a passive model overlooks many of the
advantages which civil servants possess in relation to the ministers
nominally at the head of each department.

(a) Permanence

Permanence is a key factor differentiating the civil servant from
the politician. Once appointed to office, the official has tenure.
Short of a gross misdemeanour, he cannot easily be dismissed. He
is thus, in comparison to the transitory minister, able to acquire
knowledge over a considerable period. Although civil servants
frequently change jobs they are none the less able to develop an
expertise within a particular area of policy and administration
which the minister will find difficult if not impossible to emulate.
The important point here is that departmental philosophies emerge
which provide a cultural setting within which decisions have to be
taken. The minister, especially one attempting to initiate policies
threatening the modus vivendi runs up against the weight of
accumulated departmental wisdom. For example, Barbara Castle as
Minister of Transport in 1965 saw herself surrounded by 'ill-
concealed hostility' when she attempted to introduce the idea of an
integrated transport policy. Opposition, reputedly led by the
permanent secretary Sir Thomas Padmore, was entrenched. The civil
servants had formulated alternative conceptions of appropriate
transport policy. Crossman too has indicated the extent to which
the civil service has the ability to mould attitudes and decisions
both indirectly and directly. He argued that committees of civil
servants effectively reduced the role of the Cabinet. Decisions
were prepared in advance such that it was extremely difficult for
Cabinet ministers to reach conclusions other than those determined
by officials. Further, he too reveals the pre-eminent position of
the permanent secretary. The minister is also at a distinct
disadvantage in terms of the time available to him. At most, he
is likely to remain in the department a mere two or three years.
His difficulty is that he is thus unable to command enough time to
be able to formulate, implement and monitor key policies which he
is attempting to introduce.

(b) Expertise

Time allows the civil servant to gain considerable knowledge about
the activities of the department within which he is situated. The
civil servant becomes versed in the intricacies of technical detail
within which particular policies have to be formulated and

administered. With the increase in the work of government since the
beginning of the century, more and more policy decisions have to be
made in areas in which the minister cannot expect to have developed
an expertise. Again, Crossman has pointed to the inordinately
complicated decisions which had to be made by ministers and officials
following the setting up of the Land Commission by the Labour
Government in 1964. Only the officials, and a relatively small
number of them, could hope to grasp the technical complexities of
the planning problems involved. Ministers do not serve a long
apprenticeship in their departments in a junior position as do many
managing directors in industry, but instead are catapulted into
their offices with minimal preparation. Thus it is the rare
exception to find a minister (Anthony Crosland at the Department of
Education was seen as one) who has prepared himself for the burdens
of the office which he assumes.

In this situation, the civil servant has a major part to play in
determining areas or problems in which new policies are needed.
He will be familiar with many interest groups and individuals
attempting to mould public policy in a particular area. Contacts
with outside groups are extensive and complex and are a measure of
the official's importance. Outside bodies maintain contact on a
continuous basis. Such a network of contacts provides an impressive
body of expertise upon which he can draw and which may act as an
important counterweight to ministerial opinion. This constituency
of civil servants, pressure groups and various advisory bodies may
well define the problems needing attention and the solutions
envisaged.

In addition, policy-formation and the translation of that policy
into administrative action are interlinked. New policy-making
builds on past administrative experience. It is conditioned by
what has proved to be administratively feasible or difficult. In
1964, for example, the Labour government decided to establish a
Land Commission charged with the responsibility of buying land on
which re-building was scheduled in order to bring down the price
of development land and prevent property speculation. Civil
service opinion took the view that such a policy would not bring
about the intended results due to inherent administrative difficulty.
As a result a Commission with much reduced powers of purchase
appeared on the scene. It could only charge a betterment levy on
redevelopment land. Experience in the field of planning and local
government had convinced important officials that policy should be
modified, clearly a case of civil service feedback.

(c) Administrative and organizational complexity

Decisions have become increasingly more technical with the
encroachment of government into areas such as social services,
land-use planning and civil science. Along with the growth in
complexity has come a growth in delegation of responsibility
(referred to earlier). For example, Anthony Crosland, when
Secretary of State for Education, argued that the most successful
ministers were those who concentrated on a few important issues,
leaving their civil servants to take many day-to-day decisions.

Only by limiting himself to key strategic issues could the minister hope to stamp his personality upon his department. If true of a relatively small department like Education and Science, this self-limiting strategy of ministers becomes an even more important ingredient of success in large conglomerate organizations like the Department of the Environment.

Not only is the minister governed in what he can do by the sheer volume and complexity of business; he is also effectively limited by the inherent complexity of the administrative machine. Of particular importance is the size of organization. The construction of giant departments during the 1960s and 1970s raises questions about the balance of ministerial and civil service power. In these circumstances the management of the department, nominally in the hands of the minister, must in reality pass to the civil service. The increase in the size of organizational units has inevitably led to officials having the power to decide what issues will be referred to ministers and what can be resolved without ministerial intervention.

(d) Ministerial isolation

Crossman has indicated how closetted the individual minister can become in his department subject only to the advice of his officials. Arguments for ministerial cabinets of outside advisers were strongly asserted during the 1960s in an effort to beat the dead hand of civil service orthodoxy. The Labour Party in particular was anxious to install 'temporary experts' capable of helping the minister push his policy proposals through a reluctant department. After the Labour election victory in 1974, for example, a series of special advisers were appointed by ministers to assist them in their departmental work. Thirty-eight special advisers were appointed in this manner. However, in spite of this experiment the special adviser system has not met with glowing success. Press reports indicate that since the initial appointments were made, many of these individuals have given up their jobs and moved on. There appears to be the distinct feeling in Whitehall that the permanent officials have mounted a successful campaign to ensure that the advisers are denied access to Cabinet documents and thus key information. Some came under suspicion as a result of the leak of Cabinet papers to the press. Permanent officials regard with suspicion what they see as an 'embryonic counter civil service'. With the relative failure of this experiment, the ministers are left in much the same position as before in relation to their officials: one of relative isolation.

It would be wrong to suggest that the minister is the simple yielding pawn in the hands of his senior officials. Barbara Castle was eventually able to overcome objections in the Ministry of Transport to her integrated transport plan, while Anthony Crosland has shown how he managed to reverse an extremely important decision taken by civil servants on the question of a site for the third London airport while he was at the Board of Trade. In the reminiscences and memoires of former civil servants the view is often expressed that the last thing that the civil servants in a

department welcome is a weak minister. The minister has a strong
'ambassadorial' role to play for his department. He is expected to
defend it in Cabinet discussions and to show that he is able to exert
influence in obtaining financial resources and support for his
department in the competitive bargaining involving all departments
in the battle for scarce resources. Civil servants also like a
minister with decided views and able to provide strong leadership
in the department. Nevertheless, the balance of power still remains
with permanent officials.

GOAL CONFLICT AND THE DEPARTMENT

We may assume that goal conflict in departments mirrors similar
instances of goal conflict in other organizations. These may be
considered to spring from a wide variety of causes. Two of the most
important sources of conflicts are values and perceptions.
Differences between values and perceptions may lead to conflict both
within the organization and in the relationships between it and its
environment. When such perceptual and evaluational differences
cluster around the aims of the organization or about the methods
to be used to achieve them, the conditions for goal conflict are
established.

We argued in chapter 2 that organizations do not exist in a
vacuum, but are constantly subjected to certain environmental
pressures. A goal analysis of organizations must constantly refer
to the pattern of environmental relationships binding the organization to community and society outside its boundaries. The first
place to look in an examination of goal conflict is at the pattern
of constraints imposed on the department from outside, in order to
see whether tensions may be generated as a result of competing
pressures on the department causing it to pursue goals which are
incompatible.

Demands are made, as we have seen, on the department for its
members to be accountable for their actions to parliament through
the minister. Pressures for accountability have produced a
distinct and fairly rigid bureaucratic system of administration.
But recently pressures have been generated for departments to
become more efficient in their utilization and administration of
societal resources. While the notion of bureaucracy and ministerial
responsibility is based on the values of equity and impartiality
between clients, the value of efficiency may rather demand an
organizational structure much more flexible in conception than the
bureaucratic. A new notion of accountability may have to be built
into the operational workings of a revised administrative organization.

Conflict can also arise from changes taking place within one of
these values. For example the Vehicle and General affair referred
to in chapter 2 raised important implications for the professional
conduct of civil servants and illustrates a conflict in a key value
governing their behaviour. Until recently individual civil servants
were protected by a doctrine of anonymity. But in the Vehicle and
General case the minister in charge of the department involved said
that he had no objection to individual civil servants speaking

publicly in defence of their actions. Having for many years been
protected by anonymity, civil servants are now having to readjust.
Not only are they 'named and blamed', but there has been a development
in the direction of direct answerability to the House of Commons.
Appearing as expert witnesses and giving evidence about policy-making
before parliamentary committees has modified their traditional role.
In the process some civil servants have experienced problems of
readjustment.

INTERNAL GOAL CONFLICT

Our problem in understanding conflict within departments is that
little sociological research has been done on them. Research in
this area is notoriously difficult. There are problems of access.
Experience elsewhere, however, suggests that conflict within
departments will generally assume either or both of the following
forms: first, inter-personal conflict; second, conflicts between
individuals and organizations.
     In the first of these, the question of values and perceptions is
important. Differences here provide the bedrock for conflict between
individuals and groups within the organization. A common framework
of such conflict arises when individuals and groups must work
together, but bring differences in background and outlook to their
tasks.
     We may briefly examine this kind of conflict by considering the
relationship between two groups of civil servants employed by
departments in the execution of their functions, namely generalists
and specialists. A common and frequently used distinction in the
civil service places some individuals and groups in specialist
classes, while others are treated as generalists and placed in
general administrative cadres. The assumption is made that
different kinds of knowledge are needed in the running of the
department. Essentially matters of policy and finance are seen as
the appropriate functions of generalist administrators, while
technical, scientific and professional matters are the province
of the appropriate specialist group. For over a century the civil
service has encouraged the view that the all-rounder is best suited
to the job of administration. The educational system in this
country has encouraged this. The higher levels of the civil
service have been dominated by 'Oxbridge' educated generalists.
Wide administrative experience has been seen as the best training
for high level management.
     What interests us here is what can be learnt from the conflict
between the two groups of officials in the interpretation of the
final objectives of the organization. The specialist/generalist
divide shows up a classic problem of organizations: role conflict.
Most contemporary organizations are faced with the dilemma of how
to integrate professional and non-professional workers in a
bureaucratic system. There is considerable evidence that
professionals (specialists) do not always happily co-exist with
fellow non-professional workers when the two are forced to co-operate
to achieve the goals of the organization.
     The essential problem for the civil service in this debate is

that it is still dominated by the 'cult of the generalist', the
idea that the best administrator is a gifted layman who, moving
frequently from job to job within the service, can take a practical
view of any problem in the light of his knowledge and experience
of the government machine. At the same time the tasks faced demand
the utilization of ever more specialist knowledge. The key problem
for the specialist is that he feels status deprivation compared
with the generalist. While the number of special techniques relevant
to decision-making within the public service has increased over the
last fifty years and while governments are increasingly faced with
decisions of great technical complexity, the role of the specialist
is still comparatively subordinate to that of the generalist.

The professionals have criticized the extent to which they have
been used in an advisory capacity with final decisions being taken
by generalists with inadequate expertise for evaluating the
proposals put up by the specialist. Second, compared with the
generalist administrator, the specialist has poorer career and
salary prospects. Third, the subordinate status of the specialists
prevents them exercising the full range of responsibilities
normally associated with their professions and performed by their
counterparts in industry.

For many years administrators and specialists were organized
in 'parallel' hierarchies. Under this system of organization,
financial and overall policy control was given to generalist
administrators while technical advice was made the responsibility
of the specialist. The claimed advantages of the system are that
financial control is best exercised by administrators because
specialists are not usually highly cost-conscious. Where the work
of more than one specialist group is involved necessary co-ordination
is best done by a generalist. Administrators can set specialist
matters in the context of ministerial policy and departmental
practice. On the other hand, specialists have claimed that
administrators do not have the technical competence to challenge
the financial implications of their work except on trivial points.
Second, delays and inefficiencies result from dividing responsibilities. There is also little evidence to suggest that specialists
are unsuited to the role of policy-makers.

The unification of hierarchies has occurred in certain areas of
civil service work. For example the morale of engineers in the
Ministry of Transport was reportedly low because they were kept
in the background while most important decisions were taken by
administrators. A unified hierarchy jointly headed by a deputy
secretary and professional Director of Highways and Engineering
reporting jointly to a permanent secretary was set up. In parallel
with this greater responsibility for engineering, financial and
administrative matters was delegated to divisional road engineers
(a specialist grade). The advantages of this system were that it
led to improvements in the relations between engineers and
administrators. Engineering advice became more realistic since
engineers were directly involved in policy-making and administration.

The role of generalist and specialist within the civil service
indicates that an important systems goal - the integration of
professional and generalist administrators - may be unsatisfactorily
attained from the perspective of key groups. The dominance of the

lay administrator is an arrangement that has not been adopted in
the administrations of other countries or industry to the same extent.
It is unusual for a distinction to be drawn between policy-making and
technical functions. The central issue now is whether the responsibilities of professionals should be extended so that they take full
control of the administrative and clerical work upon which they may
be engaged. Although both groups may be in agreement about the
overall objectives of the organization, there is evidence of conflict
and friction arising from competing self-images about the means
employed to reach them. The distribution of status and the
demarcation of functions between generalist and specialist is one
such axis of potential conflict within departments.

CONFLICT BETWEEN INDIVIDUALS AND ORGANIZATIONS

Personal/organizational conflict includes conflict between the
informal goals of members of the organization and its formal stated
objectives. Organizations are complex systems of human behaviour.
Civil servants are required to make decisions on the basis of
information about particular problems and choose between alternatives.
They are rational men. Since they do not act in isolation, but work
with other civil servants whose opinions they help to shape and who
in turn influence them, they are social men. They are often
motivated by considerations of morality. They are moral men. They
experience moral dilemmas over government policy from time to time.
     The civil servant will not always accept the values and norms
upon which departmental policy is constructed but may sense conflict
between his values and those of the organization. He may disagree
with the goals of the organization or the means used to achieve
them. The state of morale within the civil service will indicate
whether the organization has reached a compromise between its
goals and the economic, social and psychological needs of its
members.
     Bad morale is an indicator of personal and organizational
maladjustment. The civil service National Whitley Council (1975)
conducted a review into questions of morale. It revealed complaints
about pay and the immediate working environment. Of particular
interest was the finding that the 'ends' of departmental policy
were often questioned. Dissatisfaction was reported with constant
reversals in government policy. Successive governments had failed
to take into account the upheavals which such policy changes
inflicted on civil servants.
     Changes in departmental structure also cause problems. Government
reorganization is felt to increase impersonality and bureaucracy.
Many civil servants indicate an unwillingness to uproot themselves
and their families to resume employment in dispersed offices.
The problem of morale does show up the increasing potential for
resistance to change on the part of many civil servants. The
human relations view of organizations sensitizes us to take morale
seriously and pay heed to its consequences in any goal analysis of
the government department.

INDIVIDUAL GOALS AND ORGANIZATIONAL CHANGE

Individual needs and motivations are relevant to the success of
reorganizations designed to improve efficiency in departments. What
is known about the attitudes of civil servants to their work and the
findings of research into other organizations raises important
questions about the likely success of organizational change. The
case of accountable management illustrates this point.

Accountable management is a method of delegating authority and
resources to lower organizational levels in order to encourage
individual creativity and a sense of identity with organizational
goals. It has emerged from the widespread belief in industrial
organizations that traditional methods of motivation employing
materialistic rewards and sanctions should be replaced by a
participative style of management which would meet other human
needs such as esteem, recognition and self-actualization. This
should enable people to develop their potential more fully than in
a strictly hierarchical organization.

Such ideas stem from a group of organizational writers
concentrating on the psychological needs of individuals. Arguing
that people will only be highly motivated, and therefore productive,
when they can realize their full potential, they have recommended
the replacement of bureaucracy by a more co-operative style of
management. Representative of this thinking is Douglas McGregor
who argues for the abandonment of the 'carrot and stick' method of
management (which he calls 'Theory X') in favour of participation
and consultation ('Theory Y'). This is what Peter Drucker called
management by objectives, in contrast to management by control
(Vroom and Deci, 1970; Rose, 1978).

Accountable management in government, however, also involves a
substantial element of control. It is designed not only to
strengthen participation, but also to improve efficiency by
encouraging the clear specification of objectives, the allocation
of resources needed to meet them and the evaluation of performance
measured against agreed goals. If the emphasis is placed on the
improvement of efficiency through managerial accountability, two
possible outcomes are suggested by the results of organizational
analysis.

First, studies of civil service attitudes indicate that a more
rigorous style of management, in which career prospects are related
to performance and results, may conflict with the values that civil
servants bring to their work. Surveys have revealed that many
social and psychological, rather than meterialistic, needs are
satisfied by a civil service career, such as opportunities to
develop skills and aptitudes, the feeling of having a socially
worthwhile job and good relationships with colleagues. Accountable
management in the government context emphasizes, on the other hand,
materialistic needs and a competitive environment in which success
is rewarded and failure punished by the manipulation of salary
increments, promotion prospects and disciplinary proceedings. If
managerial change is based on false assumptions about human
motivation and individual goals it may fail. In addition, if the
members of the organization perceive such change to be out of step
with their needs they may react to it with hostility. This raises

an important dilemma. The response of management to deviation from
their objectives may be to increase supervision, thereby strengthening
central control. A management which introduces new procedures without
taking into full account individual goals runs the risk of being
obliged to strengthen the very aspects of the organization which it
strenuously wishes to reform.

Second, organizational research has shown that the delegation of
authority to subordinates may produce another undesirable consequence
for central management. Far from inducing initiative, staff may feel
reluctant to risk making errors, retreating instead to the safety of
anonymous bureaucratic procedures (Crozier, 1964).

If the emphasis in accountable management were placed more on
the autonomy and participation of staff, this may again produce two
possible outcomes. One is that it coincides with the needs and
goals of individual members. What we know of civil service motivation
suggests such an approach could be successful. The second possible
outcome, however, is that the autonomy delegated to units of
accountable management will lead to the pursuit of goals at variance
with those of the dominant coalition. Again the necessity may arise
for the organization to constrain the units to which it has delegated
power.

Whatever the approach to the delegation of authority, it cannot
be assumed that there will be congruence between individual and
organizational goals. Self-actualization theorists tend to ignore
conflict in favour of consensus, thus providing a one-dimensional
view of organization goals. While organizational analysis can
certainly inform a study of government departments, that study in
turn may act as an important corrective to some contemporary
orthodoxies within the organization theory literature itself.

Chapter 4

THE STRUCTURE OF DEPARTMENTS

The concept of a formal organization as a goal-seeking, purposive social arrangement raises many problems, not least those of structure. Organizations must be viewed at least in part as formal structures of social roles. An organization is a set of offices related to each other by rules, lines of communication and authority. Some ordering or structuring of activities is inevitable if organizational objectives are to be achieved. The relationships are prescribed in order to achieve co-operative action. They constitute definite behavioural links between the members of organizations whose roles are internally differentiated. These are the formal aspects of organizational structure as distinct from the values, conventions, practices and other behavioural regularities which spring up and attach themselves to the formal structure whenever people work together for any length of time.

Organization theory has produced a set of concepts with which to refer to the structural characteristics of organizations and which can be related to factors thought to be influential in the determination of structure. One of the most systematic attempts to conceptualize organizational structures has been made by the Industrial Administration Research Unit at Aston University. They defined six primary dimensions of organization structure: specialization, standardization, formalization, centralization, configuration and flexibility. These dimensions refer to the major structural characteristics of all organizations and permitted a comparison of a large and diverse number of organizations engaged in manufacturing, distributive and public service activities. Specialization, for example, refers to the division of labour or how official duties are distributed among a number of positions. Standardization refers to procedures governed by universal rules (Pugh et al., 1968, p.74). Formalization denotes the extent to which rules, procedures, instructions and communication are written. Centralization has to do with the level in the hierarchy where executive action can be authorized. Configuration includes the vertical span of control characteristic of the organization.

Most studies of organizational structure utilize concepts similar to these and they have an obvious relevance to many of the recommendations that are made from time to time about government

departments, though as yet there has been no systematic attempt to
measure and compare departmental structures in these terms.
This is now underway by a team of researchers at the University of
York. Nevertheless, departments have been criticized for having too
narrow spans of control, too much referral to higher authority,
insufficiently precise allocations of official responsibilities,
over-bureaucratic reliance on procedures and so on. The evidence
for such assertions is largely anecdotal, impressionistic and
fragmented. There is as yet nothing which compares to the careful
attempt by the Aston researchers to define, describe and measure
variations among a consistently applied set of structural dimensions.

Formal structures are created deliberately in order to secure the
performance of specified functions and tasks. It is therefore
legitimate to ask whether there are any factors which affect this
purposive relationship between structure and task. Can we predict
that certain tasks will require particular ways of carrying out the
necessary work if those tasks are to be performed efficiently?
There is, after all, an assumption of rationality about all
organizations in so far as they deploy their resources to achieve
the maximum effect or to produce a desired effect with the minimum
of effort. The trouble is, it is very difficult to specify
precisely what tasks need to be performed to achieve organizational
objectives because it is not always clear what those objectives
are, especially in government. So the idea of finding the best
structure of working relationships is extremely hard to put into
practice. After all, most organizations are not able to experiment
with different structures and so prove whether one is best for
their work. But it is useful to know something about formal
structure to establish its significance for other organizational
variables. However sensitive we may be to the importance of
informal social structures, or to the difficulties of measuring
organizational performance and relating it to formal structure,
we can never entirely ignore the question of whether there might
be a better way for an organization to carry out its work.

The relationship between structure and performance is particularly
important in government departments where resources are paid for
from public funds and where new objectives are constantly being set
by political leaders. Ironically, it is precisely in this group
of organizations that the problems of specification and measurement
are greatest, as we explain in our chapter on management.

THE STRUCTURAL CHARACTERISTICS OF DEPARTMENTS

From a traditional public administration perspective, government
departments are usually distinguished from other categories of
organization. Public administrative organizations are set apart
from business concerns, voluntary associations, social service
agencies and others, mainly on the grounds that they alone face
control by society generally. It is assumed that modern forms of
political control, and the constitutional separation of politics
and administration, will lead to bureaucratic structures being
found in government departments and other public sector organizations.
When we examine how departments are structured, the impact of

contemporary forms of political authority is soon revealed, although
the range of variation within each structural characteristic is
quite broad.

(a)   Accountability

First, the effect of political leadership and accountability is
apparent in the structure of departments. They are all headed by
ministers or Secretaries of State to whom powers are allocated by
law or convention and who are in turn answerable to parliament for
the administrative work performed in their departments. Ministerial
heads of departments are assisted by one or more junior ministers
(Parliamentary Secretaries or Under-Secretaries of State) and large
departments have Ministers of State to take charge of major blocks
of work while statutory authority remains vested in the senior
minister of the team. Some ministers are responsible for departments
which are nominally headed by civil servants. The Central Office of
Information, for example, is headed by a Director General and Her
Majesty's Stationery Office by a Controller, who are civil servants
of deputy secretary rank. Both departments are responsible to
Treasury ministers. The Boards of Inland Revenue and Customs and
Excise have permanent secretaries as chairmen and eight commissioners
of under-secretary rank. Both departments are responsible to the
Chancellor of the Exchequer and advise him on policy matters.

(b)   Geography

Second, although we are dealing here with organizations which are
national in scope and part of central government's administrative
machinery, their geographical coverage varies. The territorial
jurisdictions of central departments do not all correspond to the
area of the United Kingdom. So while the Foreign and Commonwealth
Office controls and administers the relations between overseas
governments and the whole of the UK, and the Board of Customs and
Excise collects and administers customs and excise duties throughout
the UK, the Department of Employment's responsibilities relating
to the use of manpower apply only to Britain. The Department of
the Environment administers the central government's functions in
relation to housing, water resources, town planning and the
supervision of local authorities generally in England alone. The
picture is complicated by the existence of Scottish and Welsh Offices,
with geographical responsibility as well as statutory functions
requiring departmental structures for those parts of the UK. It
is not necessary to go into the history which lies behind these
geographical variations. But it is important to know that
departmental functions in British central government might be
arranged along a continuum representing geographical jurisdiction.
This variable might be significant for the way departmental tasks
are performed.

(c) Size

Third, we know that we are dealing with large organizations but size is also a variable factor.
  Organization theorists have long been interested in the impact of varying size on other features of the organization particularly its structural configuration. There is now a body of empirical work concerned in particular with the relationship between size and bureaucratization. Do organizations become more bureaucratic as they grow in size? What is the relationship between size and strategies of organizational control? It has been found that the larger the organization, the greater the emphasis given to control through written rules, formal systems of communication and codified procedures. Larger size increases the complexity of organizations. There is greater division of labour and more employment of professional expertise in the larger organization. The range and frequency of repetitive occurrences increase. This requires the development of rules and procedures as an alternative to personal control by superiors of their subordinates. The volume of decisions is too great for personalized control. However, the use of experts and specialists also leads to decentralization. Professionals demand autonomy of judgment. An important study of eighty-two British companies carried out some time ago substantiated the commonly held assumption that large complex organizations tend to be bureaucratic. Size was found to exercise a dominant influence on the level of organizational complexity and this in turn affected levels of formalization and bureaucratic control. But the specialization and expertise of employees, a measure of organizational complexity, 'was an important intervening variable between the context of an organization (of which size is a key aspect) and its formalization' (Child, 1972, p.183).
  Some departments are very large, such as the Ministry of Defence with over 240,000 industrial and non-industrial civil servants. Some are relatively small by comparison, such as the Department of Education and Science with a staff of just over 3,000 or the Treasury with 1,000. The larger departments present different problems of specialization, line management, co-ordination and planning from the small departments. For example, larger departments will probably have a more decentralized system of financial control in order to avoid congestion from funnelling all transactions between spending units and the Treasury through a single finance division. Larger departments with a wide range of functions, each involving staff up to the most senior levels, may require collegiate arrangements for personnel management and budgeting. We have already noted that large departments are likely to be headed by teams of ministers, and the distribution of departmental responsibilities between members of the team for the purposes of accountability will affect the hierarchical structure below the politicians.

(d) Hierarchy

As soon as we mention hierarchy we come to a fourth variable and one of the distinguishing characteristics of bureaucratic organiza-

tions generally and government departments in particular. A
bureaucracy consists essentially of a hierarchy of offices, each
clearly under the supervision of a higher office. Each office in
the hierarchy has a fixed jurisdiction laid down according to the
laws and regulations which the organization is required to administer.
The power of the official is thus legal and rational. What the
official may or may not do is specified by the rules of the office
held. Authority is totally impersonal and instrumental. This
applies to both the way in which personnel are recruited to fill
bureaucratic offices and to the way in which officials apply
bureaucratic rules to particular cases. Government departments
are characterized by very strict hierarchy. Below the ministerial
level, responsibility for administration and finance is concentrated
in the authority of the department's most senior administrator, its
permanent secretary. Departments tend to have tall, narrow pyramidal
hierarchies with limited spans of control. In some cases only two
or three subordinates report to a senior officer, and there may be
as many as nine organizational levels. A combination of factors
has produced this feature of departmental organization. Some are
related to the requirements of parliamentary accountability, such
as the need for detailed checks to be made of financial transactions.
Others derive from the need to maintain continuity with frequent
movements of staff. Work tends to be broken down into small,
specialized jurisdictions which occupy small numbers of officials.
The structure of the civil service and its grading system is also
influential in that the organizational hierarchy has to correspond
to the number of civil service ranks within different occupational
groups.

The effect of such hierarchy has been to clarify the line of
command, while at the same time diffusing authority so that it is
rarely possible to identify the point at which decisions are taken.
Responsibility tends to be blurred. Departments have been advised
to adopt flatter pyramids with broader spans of control. Organizational structures, it is rightly said, should follow from tasks
and not personnel grading systems. Reducing the number of working
levels should enable authority to be allocated more precisely.
A department could then be reconstructed around a number of budget
centres or accountable units having precisely defined objectives
so that performance can be measured, costed and evaluated (see
chapter 3). Each unit would be held responsible for achievement
and efficiency would thereby be enhanced. The Fulton Committee
originally spoke of 'commands', the managers of which being given
'clear-cut responsibilities and commensurate authority and being
held accountable for performance against budgets, standards of
achievement and other tests' (Fulton, 1968, para.154).

The application of accountable management principles in central
government has led to extensive changes being made to the structure
of some government departments. These changes represent a
compromise between the traditional departmental structure and a
highly decentralized system of administration in which whole blocks
of executive work are delegated to quite separate agencies,
sometimes known as 'hiving off'. This compromise has entailed the
creation of departmental agencies which, though part of the
department, enjoy more autonomy in financial and managerial matters

than other parts. Important and varied functions of government have
been managed in this way, including defence procurement, government
property services, ordnance factories, naval dockyards and employment
services. Nearly 200,000 civil servants work in them, or approximately 26 per cent of the civil service (Jordan, 1976).

Where it has been decided that a departmental agency is an
appropriate organizational response it has been for one of two main
reasons. First, the work involves a form of commercial trading, but
under the special circumstances in which the government itself is
the major customer - ordnance production, dockyards, government
supplies, for example. Here the agencies levy charges to finance
current expenditure and borrow to finance capital development. They
are not dependent on the department's annual votes. However, their
position cannot be all that different from other parts of the
department since their commercial relations with their 'customers'
are somewhat notional. They cannot refuse to sell. They cannot
charge the market price. Their 'bills' are ultimately paid from
departmental votes. The kind of managerial attitudes generated by
the need to set targets and performance indicators could also be
generated by similar practices in other sections of the department.
The setting of priorities and the collection of relevant information
for management is not exclusive to departmental agencies.

Second, agencies have been set up for routine executive operations.
Their autonomy is even more notional than those with trading funds.
They are open to all forms of ministerial intervention. They have
to conform to departmental standards and policies on recruitment,
pay, promotion and conditions. In their actual operations they are
difficult to distinguish clearly from the traditional form of
departmental management. There is no guarantee that they will be
free to control the factors affecting performance, or that there
will be no politically motivated interventions in their management.
In government the practice of management, as well as decisions
about managerial structures, reflects political compromises and
objectives. Degrees of managerial autonomy do not, in central
government at least, correlate neatly with managerial structure.
A structural continuum, ranging from complete integration within
the formal departmental hierarchy at one extreme, to a hived-off
status at the other, is unlikely to be matched by parallel
variations in managerial autonomy. The political sensitivity of
an executive activity rarely corresponds exactly to organizational
forms.

The feeling that the clear location of managerial responsibility
is difficult within the traditional departmental structure has
become so strong in some cases that special executive agencies have
been set up outside their original departments (hiving off).
Indeed, the Department of Employment has been virtually dismembered,
with its staff fragmented into five separate organizations. One
of these, the Employment Services Agency, was created because of
failures within the department to respond adequately to the demands
of the labour market and to plan ahead. A new and quite separate
structure was thought necessary to assign responsibility to a
clear line of management throughout the organization. This is
how the first chief executive of the Agency, himself a senior civil
servant, described the effects of the old structure (Cooper, 1975):

When I was appointed we had for the first time in thirty if not sixty years somebody at the head of the Employment Service with well defined responsibilities for its ongoing performance and operation, for the development of those services according to assessed needs, and for the optimal use of resources. It amazes me that for a generation at lease we had been running those services in such a way that there was nobody below the Permanent Secretary in the Department with specific and total responsibility for the efficiency and effectiveness of them...   This was one part of the problem. For the rest we had the traditional civil service system of management which I have characterized or sometimes described as management by default. You had on the one hand the policy makers, the mandarins, full of bright ideas but rarely getting at very close quarters with the service in the market place, sending out streams of instructions without having a clear appreciation of their impact on the organization or consistent view of its priorities. More important still they had no direct responsibility whatever for the way in which resources were used. On the other hand of course you had all the heirs of Gladstone; the establishment officers, the finance officers responsible for safeguarding public resources without any direct responsibility for carrying out programmes. What that so often meant was that we should do things cheaply rather than that we should use the resources that we'd got as well as we ought in relation to the objectives that we were setting out to achieve.... Traditionally there has been a lack of operational flexibility, difficulty in switching planned expenditures to meet changes of circumstances arising during the financial year, partly because we did not know how much money was attributable to the employment service, partly because money had to be carried on so many different votes and partly because moving money between sub-heads in the DE Vote normally required specific authority from the Treasury. In such circumstances quick responses to unforeseen changes are made the exception rather than the rule.

These changes reveal very clearly two conflicting principles of accountability at work and, therefore, the structural contradictions generated by the political environment of central government. Departmental agencies were used in place of hiving off because the political and administrative heads of the departments concerned were not prepared to release the executive work from close ministerial or budgetary control. It is ultimately a matter of political judgment, rather than any objective circumstances of a particular area of administration, as to whether the work should remain in the traditional departmental hierarchy, be delegated to a departmental agency or hived off to a separate organization with a quasi-autonomous management.

(e) Specialization

We have already alluded to the fact that work has to be broken down into segments which can be allocated to units and individuals. This is in fact the next characteristic of bureaucracy - speciali-

zation. Large-scale organizations are inevitably multi-functional
in that the activities needed to achieve objectives have to be
distributed among different individuals and groups in manageable
proportions and according to the different skills and abilities
needed to do the work. Specialization is given a new dimension in
a government department which has a number of different policies
and laws to administer, some of which may only be distantly related
to others. For example, a single ministry may be responsible for
sponsoring the engineering and vehicles industries, reorganizing
the merchant shipbuilding industry, developing atomic energy policy,
supporting the aircraft and aerospace industries, procuring aircraft
and electronic equipment for defence purposes and encouraging
technological development in industry generally.

Such a department would be divided into a small number of
directorates or commands, say for engineering, research and aviation.
Each group would be in the charge of a civil servant of deputy
secretary rank answerable to the ministry's permanent secretary.
A directorate in which work is of a highly technical nature might
be under the joint control of an administrator and a senior engineer
of equal status. If the work is exclusively scientific research
the chief officer is likely to be the head of the department's
professional scientific staff. A directorate will consist of a
number of divisions each headed by an under-secretary or equivalent
professional civil servant. So the engineering group, for example,
might be divided into divisions for industrial policy, international
and technological manpower, economic and statistical analysis and
divisions for each of the groups of industries for which the
department has some responsibility.

As work is further broken down into specialisms, so the structure
will be further segmented into branches under an assistant secretary
or equivalent. For example, one of the divisions in the aviation
directorate might be divided into branches handling the export
promotion of defence equipment, each branch specializing in either
military aircraft, military hovercraft, guided weapons or military
electronic equipment.

Every department also has to have its common services divisions.
There will be a finance division advising the permanent secretary
as accounting officer. This division will be responsible for the
preparation of expenditure plans to be submitted to the Treasury
and parliament each year in the form of Estimates. It will also
perform the central accounting and payment duties of the department.
A finance division consults with the policy, or 'spending',
divisions and converts the department's forecasts of financial
needs into annual estimates of current and capital expenditure.
These are discussed in detail with the Treasury. Reports on the
cost of continuing current policies, analyses of expenditure
forecasts for other services, and commentaries on Treasury forecasts
of economic changes are submitted to the minister. After Cabinet
and committee meetings to settle expenditure limits, the finance
division applies Cabinet decisions to departmental estimates and,
where appropriate, the forecasts of other agencies such as public
corporations and local authorities. Increasingly, the work of
planning financial allocations supersedes in importance the traditional functions of finance divisions, namely ensuring proper cash

accounting and guarding against the improper use of funds. 'Economy' in departmental expenditure is now more likely to mean the measurement of efficiency in terms of the resources needed to produce different types and levels of 'output', rather than simply keeping the cost of any activity as low as possible.

Another common service found in all departments is that of personnel management usually organized by an establishments and management services division. Such a division might, in a large department, have two under-secretaries at its head, one responsible for staff matters such as deployment and training (the principal establishment officer) and another for organization and methods, office services, automatic data processing and other management aids and techniques.

(f)   Decentralization

We have referred to the geographic scope of departmental responsibilities. The fact that departments administer functions for the whole society and that their client groups are not geographically concentrated means that the principles of hierarchy and specialization have to be extended geographically until a decentralized administrative structure is formed. Decentralization involves the territorial delegation of authority to departmental officers. The phenomenon is a very familiar one, and it is often this part of a department's organization which is most familiar to the individual citizen. The reasons for this become obvious when we consider the tasks performed by decentralized offices. (Decentralization should not be confused with the dispersal of headquarters units from London, or with the 'central' departments serving the Secretaries of State for Scotland and Wales.)

The administrative structure of decentralization requires a geographical division of the country into areas which are appropriate to the tasks to be delegated. The range of such divisions is potentially very great. Tax districts, for example, reflect the work load generated by the assessment and collection tasks of the Inland Revenue, and will consequently create a different administrative map to the social security areas of the Department of Health and Social Security. The DHSS has approximately 800 local offices, each providing a point of contact between the department and the clients generated by a given size of population. Different areas again will be required for the DES or Home Office inspectorates, the Department of the Environment's planning regions or road transport divisions, and the Ministry of Agriculture's advisory services and inspectorates. Some departments need an elaborate hierarchy of multiple levels of decentralization, such as MAFF, which has both regional and divisional land commissioners, veterinary officers and executive staff. Some departments have more than one decentralized structure (the Department of the Environment at one time had thirteen).

Each regional, area or local office must be placed under a controller, director or manager who in turn will be supported by staffs of administrators and specialists. Two-thirds of the civil service are employed in regional and local offices, a proportion

which, of course, hides variations between departments. The tasks
they perform are as varied as the functions of the departments in
which they are situated.

One task of decentralized officials is the direct administration
of a service to the general public or the enforcement of an obligation
on the public (such as social security payments or revenue collection)
where a face-to-face relationship with the department's clients or
claimants is required. Officials simply must be on the spot to deal
with claims for government services, whether they be supplementary
benefits, industrial development certificates or agricultural grants,
when and where they are made. Another administrative function which
also calls departmental officials into the field is the supervision
of subordinate agencies, such as local councils and health authorities.
Here the administrative function has to be decentralized in order to
provide geographical and technical specialization and ease of access.
Central departments are involved here in a range of activities:
inspection (schools, police forces, fire brigades, factories),
advice (town planning for example) and control (such as applications
for slum clearance or housing programmes). In all cases decentralized
staff act as the eyes and ears of the department, advising headquarters
and the policy-makers on local developments, new policy requirements
and the reactions of affected interests. They provide an important
channel of communication between the centre and the field.

The bureaucratic characteristics of hierarchy and specialization
create the familiar form of organization whose structure can be
represented in diagrammatic form as in Figures 4.1, 4.2 and 4.3.
For illustrative purposes we have chosen a reorganized structure
proposed for the Inland Revenue by a management review committee
in 1975 since it shows clearly the effects of the features we have
described. Figure 4.2 shows how a typical division or branch might
look and is thus an extension of Figure 4.1, though not from the
same department. Figure 4.3 is an example of a regional organization
employing a wide range of professional staff.

THE VARIABILITY OF TASKS

No government department is identical to another. There are structural
variations in respect of all the elements of departmental organization
we have mentioned. Yet there are some remarkable similarities given
the wide range of administrative, professional and technical tasks
which have to be performed. If these tasks are as diverse as they
appear then it would seem as if structure is determined by other
factors which have the effect of bringing about organizational
uniformity across a range of government departments and ministries.
On the face of it the following departmental responsibilities have
little in common: the provision and management of office accommodation
(Directorate of Home Estate Management, Department of the Environment);
national insurance scheme benefits (Insurance Division B of DHSS); the
Explosives Branch of the Fire Department of the Home Office; student
awards (Universities Branch of DES); or policy for recruiting,
training, licensing, certifying and staffing Air Traffic Control
(the Directorate of Air Traffic Control, Controllerate of National
Air Traffic Services, Department of Trade and Industry). Yet the

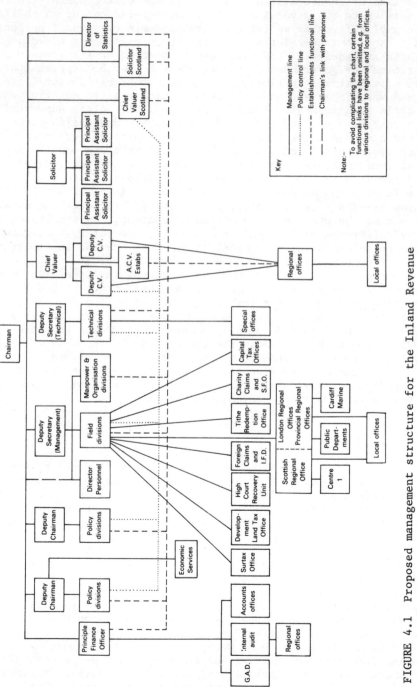

FIGURE 4.1 Proposed management structure for the Inland Revenue

Source: Inland Revenue Management Review, 'Proposals of the Review Committee for the Structure of the Department', January 1975.

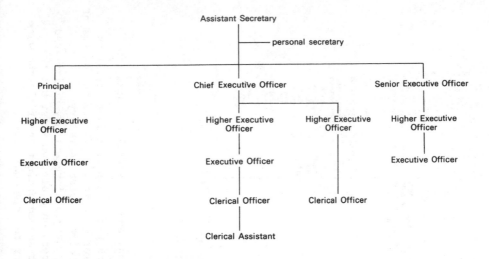

FIGURE 4.2 A typical division

organizational structures for these functions are very similar.
The problem for us is that we do not know what activities, tasks and
processes of decision-making are needed before these broad and
somewhat vague responsibilities can be performed. Unfortunately
we know very little about these activities apart from the fact that
they generate a great deal of written records and committee
meetings. We are not yet able to classify tasks to see if some
formal structures might be more conducive to organizational success
than others. We can, however, suggest some distinctions and
categories which might be starting points and which, in any event,
reveal more of the structural features which are the subject of
this chapter.
   One way in which the functions of departments vary is in whether
they administer some policy direct to the public or client group,
or alternatively are charged with the supervision, control or
guidance of other executive agencies, such as public corporations
and local authorities, which deliver the service to the public.
However, with the trend towards large organizations created by the
amalgamation of smaller ministries, few departments now have no
responsibilities for subordinate bodies as well as their direct
executive functions. Two departments created in 1970 and since
modified illustrate this. The Department of Trade and Industry was
created by the merger of the Ministry of Technology and Board of
Trade. It became responsible for the direct administration of the
Secretary of State's powers in relation to industry and commerce,
including tariffs, company law, monopolies, mergers, export
promotion and credit, advisory services to small and medium size
firms and regional industrial development. The department also had
to administer the government's relations with a number of public
industrial corporations and research establishments which introduced
an element of indirect administration into the organization. The
Department of the Environment brought together three ministries:
Public Buildings and Works, mainly concerned with the provision of

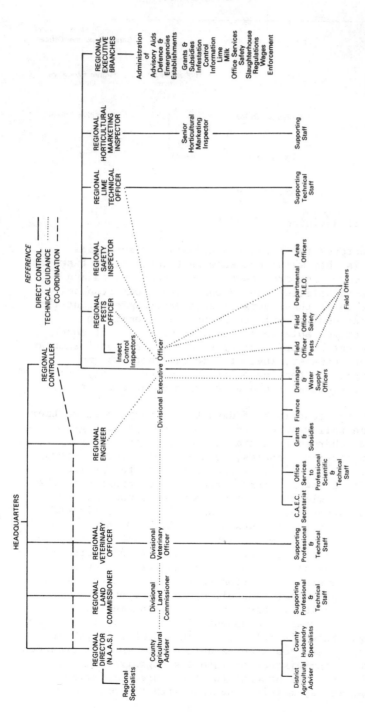

FIGURE 4.3   Ministry of Agriculture, Fisheries and Food: typical regional and divisional organization

Notes: 1   There are eight regions in England and Wales: on average each region contains four divisions. A division consists of one large county or two or more smaller counties. In Wales the duties of regional controller have been added to the responsibilities of the Welsh Secretary.

2   The regional director (N.A.A.S.), regional land commissioner, regional veterinary officer and regional drainage engineer report independently to headquarters on their own work, but the regional controller is responsible for the general oversight and co-ordination of all the work in the region and for a wide range of establishment functions for regional staff.

office accommodation and other buildings for the civil service and
armed forces; Housing and Local Government, concerned with the
control of local authorities in general and some of their specific
functions in particular; and Transport, which combined both executive
and supervisory functions in its highways programme and its relations
with local highways authorities and the nationalized transport
industries.

A second contrast in terms of function which might be made is
between departments responsible for policies and services for
public consumption, such as education, police or welfare, and
departments providing services to central government itself – the
common service departments of the state, as it were.   One major
common service – the management of public property – happens to be
the responsibility of a department which also has policy functions,
as we have already seen.   A further complication is that 'common
service' is a very broad category, encompassing the provision of
services, such as public information (COI), legal services and staff
training, as well as co-ordinating mechanisms such as the Treasury
and Civil Service Department.   The problem of the range and variety
of functions assigned to the 'spending' departments also remains.

Yet another distinction that can be drawn is between the
administrative, managerial and professional work carried out in
government departments.   Often the segmentation of departments into
divisions and branches reflects these differences.   The work of
administrative divisions can be grouped into four broad areas.
First there is financial planning and control.   This includes
expenditure forecasting, usually over a four-year period, and the
application of financial controls over the work of the department,
including sections staffed by engineers, architects and other
professionals.   Second, administrative work means policy development.
Administrative divisions are usually responsible for the development
of new policies, from the preparation and circulation of draft
papers on the initial proposal, to the drafting of a Bill in those
cases where new legislation is required.   This work usually requires
extensive consultation with non-departmental bodies, such as local
authorities and public corporations, and with private concerns, such
as industrial organizations and interest groups.   Participation on
departmental and interdepartmental committees is an important
feature of administrative work in the development of new policies.
It has been estimated that a third of all administrators spend at
least a quarter of their time on committee work.

Then there is case work.   The administration of policy generates
a case-load of individual decisions that have to be taken by
administrators.   The individual cases thrown up by legislation are
often extremely complex and politically sensitive.   They may become
cases which ministers have to decide on, and administrators then
become involved in preparing explanatory briefs and in drafting
answers to parliamentary questions or the minister's correspondence.
Explanations of departmental policies generally may have to be
provided to other departments, outside organizations or parliamentary
committees.   Material supporting the minister's political work,
such as parliamentary speeches, also has to be provided by administrative divisions.

Management in government involves some administrative divisions

in the supervision of large blocks of staff dealing with such
matters as social security records and contracts. Establishment
divisions are also usually staffed at the higher levels by
administrators. But it is in this general category of work that the
distinction between administrative and executive work begins to break
down. Posts in divisions such as these are staffed by administrators
mainly because of the seniority required. Also, with the integration
of the former administrative and executive classes (see chapter 5),
it is more difficult to distinguish purely administrative and
executive divisions.

'Management' generally refers to the work of executive branches
which is of a more routine kind and where the policy implications of
decisions are less in evidence. The management of contracts, social
security records, stores units and accounting branches, for example,
requires large numbers of executive and clerical staff in separate
organizational hierarchies working under administrative personnel.
An example of this on a large scale is the national insurance records
office of the Department of Health and Social Security. Here some
10,000 staff are organized in three divisions (one is Establishments
and Organization) and seven branches. These branches maintain
records of the contributions paid by all insured persons, issue
payments books to those receiving long-term benefits and family
allowances, draw up the accounts for the payments made by local
offices of the department, and keep records of all long-term
beneficiaries. The office handles about nine million claims for
sickness benefit and four million for unemployment and maternity
allowances each year.

All departments now have to employ professionally qualified
specialists such as accountants, economists, engineers, surveyors,
architects and different categories of scientist. The organization
of 'specialists' (as distinct from 'generalists') within departments
has produced many problems and attracted a good deal of criticism
from time to time (see chapter 3). Specialists give advice on the
technical merits of proposals and take charge of the technical work
itself, such as the planning and design of motorways, the design
and supervision of school buildings and the construction of naval
works.

TASK AND STRUCTURE

There has been no systematic research of a comparative nature
designed to classify and analyse departmental work processes in order
to identify the most appropriate structures for different tasks.
Organization and methods studies are, of course, frequently carried
out into the work of sections within departments, subjecting them to
various tests derived from management theory and operations research.
But these one-off reviews, when they lead to change, do not tell us
whether the organization performs better as a result of structural
reorganization or, if it does, whether this is because of the
restructuring or some other factor which might have produced the
same effects without change in the structure.

Beyond this, however, there has been very little done even in the
way of speculation to see if different tasks need significantly

different structures. The division of central government into very
broad functions, commonly found in the literature on public
administration, such as foreign affairs, economic and industrial
policy, law and order and social services, tells us nothing about
the appropriate management structures for the departments involved.
Attention has concentrated in the past on the macro-level of the
machinery of government. This obscures the variety of tasks being
performed within any one function or department. It is not even a
useful guide to the way ministerial powers should be distributed
among the organizations of central government.

An alternative which is more relevant to the problem of structure
is to divide the activities of central departments into 'operative'
and 'adaptive/creative' administration (Baker, 1972). The
'operative' functions of departments are those involving the
application of laws, regulations or policies within well defined
procedures and objectives. Discretion is limited and work processes
are routine. The kind of organizational structure required is
likely to be mechanistic, corresponding closely to the classic
bureaucratic form with specialization of function, hierarchical
lines of authority, limited discretion and emphasis placed on the
value of experience in the work of the department. Baker suggests
that such a structure might be appropriate to departmental tasks
involving regulation - whether of individuals, firms, corporations
or local authorities - within a clearly defined legal framework
and with only limited discretion available to officials.

The most obvious example is the social security work of awarding
and paying benefits, collecting contributions, visiting claimants
and interviewing callers. In the Department of Health and Social
Security it was found that the regional management structure was
weak because of the absence of a clear management link between
local and regional offices. Local office managers were subject to
direction by as many as six or more specialists with functional
responsibilities at regional level which involved them in some
management aspects of local office work. At the same time, regional
controllers could not be held accountable for the work of any local
office as a whole or for the overall performance of a region when
the number of local offices in a region ranged from 50 to 127. So
a new tier had to be inserted in the hierarchy by dividing local
offices into groups accountable to a group manager. A specialist
could then advise their group managers but not direct local office
managers. There was, in effect, a need to clarify lines of command,
develop narrower and more specific responsibilities and add new
levels to the organizational hierarchy - all examples of greater
bureaucratization.

'Adaptive/creative' functions relate to the making, altering and
adapting of government policies through new laws and regulations.
It might be argued that policy-making requires much less clearly
defined areas of responsibility and less formal interaction between
individuals and groups. The type of structure which might be
expected to emerge here would be organic. Administrative activity
would be structured to co-ordinate work so that different kinds of
information, from technical facts to political values, could be
assimilated. Functional responsibilities would not be precisely
defined. Differences of rank would be less important than differences

of expertise (teamwork rather than hierarchy). Communication, whether vertical, horizontal or diagonal, would be more important than lines of command. Such an organization might be appropriate for expenditure forecasting, reviewing investment programmes of government agencies such as the nationalized industries, preparing legislation and negotiating with outside bodies. Departmental research and development activities would also be organized in loose, organic structures in which project team members would have considerable freedom to define their own tasks.

The distinction between operative and adaptive organizations is too crude to be a great deal of use in designing organizational structures. It may lead to the acceptance of a false dichotomy between policy and administration. Many units within government departments carry out work which has both regulative and creative components. The categorization may leave some administrative processes unaccounted for. Nevertheless, it has the virtue of warning against the acceptance of any single model of management structure for government departments.

As a typology, it corresponds to a distinction observed by organization theorists concerned with the different environments to which organizations have to respond. The focus here has been on the volatility of the economic and technological circumstances affecting particular firms or industries. For example, Burns and Stalker (1961) carried out a study of twenty electronics firms in the early 1960s and encountered a variety of forms of management structure. These they grouped into two, the mechanistic and the organic.

The mechanistic model corresponds closely to Weberian bureaucracy. It is characterized by task specialization, the precise definition of duties and responsibilities, vertical and clearly defined patterns of communication, and hierarchically centralized control mechanisms. The mechanistic system of management was the most appropriate for firms operating under relatively stable market conditions. Routine behaviour is an efficient way of handling unchanging tasks.

The organic system was found to be more suitable for a rapidly changing product environment. Here there is a continuous need to innovate in order to deal with new and unpredictable problems. The organic model had no clearly defined hierarchy. Roles were continually redefined. Co-ordination depended heavily on lateral communication, especially verbal, in management committees. These were characterized by the exchange of advice and information rather than the issuing of instructions. Little attention was paid to organization charts, formal job descriptions or hierarchical status. The organic system was more concerned with mobilizing expert knowledge than with breaking work down into distinct and discrete tasks. It had developed a greater capacity than the mechanistic system to handle information in a way that was highly adaptive in the face of new problems.

A similar response to environmental variation was observed by Lawrence and Lorsch in their study of firms in the plastics, container and consumer food industries. The successful firms in each industry were those which maintained appropriate organizational responses, in terms of differentiation and integration, to the technical and economic conditions outside the organization. For example, the plastics industry had to survive in an environment where new

products and processes were being developed and where the future was
highly uncertain. Uncertainties also surrounded the scientific
knowledge required to meet customers' demands for new products.
However, other areas of the environment were more predictable.
Successful firms were those which produced a differential response
from their departments - sales, production, research and so on -
consistent with the requirements of their own sub-environments. For
example, production units had the most formalized structures - more
levels in the managerial hierarchy, a higher ratio of supervisors to
subordinates and more specific reviews of departmental and individual
performance than the other departments. The environment of production
managers required more established routines and tighter controls.
Lawrence and Lorsch concluded that

> the high-performing organization came nearer to meeting the
> demands of its environment than its less effective competitors.
> The most successful organizations tended to maintain states of
> differentiation and integration consistent with the diversity
> of the parts of the environment and the required interdependence
> of these parts. (Lawrence and Lorsch, 1967, p.134)

Firms and other organizations in real life do not fall neatly
into distinct categories. They vary in the degree to which they
exhibit all the features of a particular model. One of the most
interesting features of the Burns and Stalker study, particularly
for students of government departments, is their description of the
behaviour of mechanistic organizations trying to cope with unfamiliar
market conditions and other changes in their environment. In their
efforts to make their bureaucratic systems work they tended to
reinforce the rigorously defined roles and working relationships
of the formal structure. Consequently, they tended to develop what
Burns and Stalker described as 'pathological' forms of the
mechanistic system. The pathological systems which resulted are very
reminiscent of government departments struggling to cope with new
tasks in a changing political environment with the structural and
managerial traditions deriving from earlier forms of state intervention and administrative function: the reference of unfamiliar
problems to higher and higher levels, the proliferation of structures
and specialisms to deal with the new problems and the use of
committees to deal with tasks for which no individual is suited.

TECHNOLOGY AND STRUCTURE

In central government we are faced with a bewildering array of
management tasks, some of which have their counterparts in the
private sector, such as financial planning and accounting, and some
have not, such as processing planning appeals or regulating consumer
credit and environmental pollution. These tasks have to be performed
in fields of administration which sometimes bear a resemblance to
some private organizations because they are of a commercial and
productive character, such as the ordnance factories of the Ministry
of Defence, and which sometimes do not, such as the management of
prisons. The variety of administrative tasks is so great that it
is difficult for students of organizations to know how to handle it.
One way is to try and adapt the concept of technology as used in
organization theory to relate structure to tasks.

The classification of organizations according to the technologies
of the productive process was attempted in the private manufacturing
sector by Joan Woodward in her book 'Industrial Organization' (1965).
She found that successful firms had management structures which were
close to the norm for those using a given productive process, whether
it be unit production, 'small batch' production, mass production or
process production. The further a firm moved away from the structure
appropriate to its technology, the less chance it had of being
successful as measured by such indicators as market shares and
labour turnover. Other studies of business organizations have shown
that technological variables are associated with structures relating
to role specialization, functional specialization and other activities
closely associated with the main workflow. Size is also important,
since the relationship between technological and structure variables
sometimes appears stronger in smaller organizations (Child and
Mansfield, 1972).

Some attempts have been made to apply the concept of technology
to non-industrial and public service organizations, but as yet it
remains to be seen whether there might be any correlation within
central departments between efficiency, structure and 'technology'
or process of decision-making. However, an interesting attempt to
extend the concept of technological implications beyond the manufacturing sector has been made by the American sociologist Charles
Perrow (1970).

By technology Perrow means the actions which an administrator
performs upon 'objects' (the interaction of individuals; the
processing of documents; material resources such as money or
equipment) in order to change them. The structure of an organization
is then defined as the form which is taken by the interaction of
administrators or managers for the purpose of making such changes.
Structures are expressed as methods of co-ordination, spans of
control, types and degrees of delegation, personnel ratios and so
on.

Technology has two dimensions. The first is the number of
exceptional cases or the variety of problems which have to be dealt
with by an administrative process. So the decision-making process
will vary according to whether the organization is faced with many
or few familiar situations. The second dimension Perrow calls the
'search process' which refers to methods of analysing and solving
problems arising in the pursuit of organizational objectives. Some
problems are immediately subject to known methods of analysis and
little judgment or discretion is required before a solution can be
found. Others may require processes of analysis which have to be
specially devised because the problem cannot be fitted into one of
the available methods of problem solving. Perrow illustrates this
by a two-dimensional grid which brings the two continua of 'number
of exceptional cases' and 'the degree to which search procedures
are analysable' together, giving four types of decision-making
technology: craft, non-routine, routine and engineering (see
Figure 4.4).

Perrow's hypotheses concerning the relationships between
technology and structure have received some empirical support in
the public sector by a small amount of American research, but have
not been tested in the context of British central government. Yet

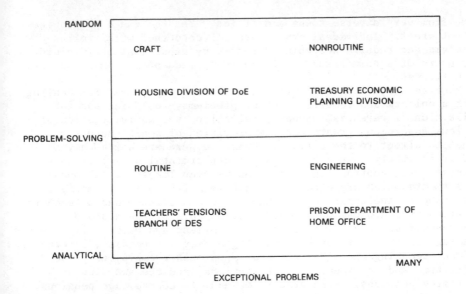

FIGURE 4.4 Perrow's technology

Adapted from C. Perrow, 'Organizational Analysis. A Sociological
View', Tavistock Publications, London 1970.

the variety of administrative tasks would seem to warrant more
complex analysis than has been carried out by critics of departmental
organization, such as the Fulton Committee's investigation of the
civil service some years ago. It is not at this stage possible to
group departmental tasks in any way definitively under the four
headings suggested by Perrow's dimensions of technology, but even
a superficial glance at the work of government departments indicates
that the typology has some relevance.

   Craft technologies for solving familiar problems without
standardized techniques of problem-solving have their counterparts
in government work on accounting, auditing and the control of
expenditure. The administration of controls over the public
corporations – prices, capital investment, research programmes and
general economic policy for the public sector – would also come
under this heading. Indeed, work on the supervision of subordinate
bodies in the administrative system often seems to take on the
characteristics of problem-solving which is non-routine and requiring
judgment rather than reference to fixed rules and regulations which
prescribe action for all cases. But at the same time, the problems
facing the organizations involved are relatively familiar. So the
departments situated in this part of the matrix are likely to be
clustered near its centre. The work of one of the housing divisions
of the Department of the Environment illustrates this. Clearance
orders and compulsory purchase orders by local authorities dealing
with unfit houses need ministerial confirmation. The division has
to exercise varied powers requiring considerable discretion as to
whether houses have been correctly described as unfit or whether the
orders should be confirmed wholly, in part, or rejected. The orders

come from very diverse towns and cities. Yet the range of problems is not great. Individual orders are all concerned with similar problems and require searching scrutiny by departmental officials on the basis of a common and consistently applied policy on standards of unfitness.

Routine administration, with standardized procedures for dealing with a uniform and recurring set of problems, would include the collection of revenues, property valuation, the administration of various government grants and the provision of social security benefits direct to the citizen. Examples here are quite easy to find, and it is likely that a good deal of departmental work falls within this sector. Routine administration is even likely to be found in departments which are otherwise concerned with policy formation. For example, the Department of Education and Science has a teachers' pensions branch whose work covers all aspects of the statutory superannuation scheme for teachers in England and Wales. It involves the investigation of service and eligibility for pension, interchanges between teaching and other kinds of pensionable employment, the collection and repayment of contributions, and the awarding of infirmity pensions, death gratuities and, of course, age pensions. Much of the work is quantifiable and standardized. Not surprisingly it is organized in traditional hierarchical style.

Non-routine administration occurs when there are many unique problems to be solved but where 'search procedures' are unanalysable. In government this would include long-term policy planning in all fields, together with environmental and economic planning, such as reorganizing public transport in the conurbations or producing medium-term projections of the British economy. It would also include short-term projects, such as the preparation of ministerial speeches, and the formulation of administrative procedures for handling case-work on social security claims, compensation schemes and town and country planning appeals. The management of research and development would also require this type of decision-making. The Treasury's work of co-ordinating economic policy is also characterized by widely varying problems and non-routine methods of problem-solving. The work is almost wholly advisory in that it involves collation, analysis and appraisal. The 'products' of the planning divisions are reports, surveys and studies of particular problems. These may be specially commissioned studies of domestic and international economic problems, or economic forecasts. The structure for organizing this work includes the integration of professional economists and administrative personnel.

The engineering technology, where tasks are varied but problem-solving procedures are relatively routinized, includes the management of computer installations, the preparation of legislation and statutory instruments, the minister's parliamentary work (questions, correspondence, briefs for debates and so on) and establishment work (training, staff inspection, postings, promotions and the application of management techniques). The Prison Department of the Home Office is a policy division where the nature of the problems to be solved is very varied but where the procedures for solving them are fairly precisely prescribed by law. The department has to direct each person sentenced by the courts to a period of detention to an establishment most appropriate to his security classification. This consideration has also to be combined with other unique characteristics of the prisoner, such as the treatment or training required and the location of his family. The department has also to provide medical, religious, educational and recreational facilities. But at the same time, prisoners have to be treated equally under current legislation. So the department has to react to social, economic and demographic trends in the community regardless of the economics of particular policies. It has to respond to a 'demand' which is outside its control. The structure of the department consequently has to combine clear lines of managerial authority with integrated teams of professionals and administrators for the inspection of custodial institutions and planning to meet long-term needs. There is a high degree of internal differentiation varying from the traditional scalar hierarchy for the processing of routine transactions to more flexible, organic structures for research and development tasks in which project team members have considerable freedom to define their own roles.

Though it is not possible to see different structures being adopted for different decision-making technologies – the pressures towards homogeneity are very powerful – it is possible to recognize within a single department the different categories of problem-solving identified here. In the old Department of Employment, for example, there were divisions concerned with employment policy which were wholly non-routine, giving advice on manpower questions, studying the employment implications of new town developments and overspill schemes, producing information on national, regional and local employment trends and advising on distribution of industry policy and the local employment Acts. Then there was the 'craft' work of the employment service, including the placement work of the employment exchanges, occupational guidance and the placing of redundant workers. There was the more routine work of implementing the Selective Employment Payments Act and dealing with appeals. And finally there was work which appeared to be of an 'engineering' type, such as personnel management and accounting. Perhaps the subsequent dismantling of the department into separate agencies reflects the different problem solving it had to perform.

Obviously few administrative tasks are confined to one category exclusively and it is often necessary in government to integrate the structures dealing with long-term planning, the preparation of legislation and case-work arising from the administration of existing policy. Indeed, the concept of technology is a difficult one to apply to government departments precisely because technology and structure are so closely interwoven. This is because what the administrative process 'produces' cannot be separated from the structural context within which 'production' takes place. If the product is a decision, the technology of producing it can only be explained in terms of social relationships – in other words structures of management.

We are reminded here of a reservation about the concept of technology expressed by Woodward herself, when she asked whether a control system is yet another dimension of technology. Rose suggests that it is. 'One result is some logical difficulty with the whole thesis: the proposition that organization varies with technology is less arresting in so far as technology *equals* organization, and vice versa' (Rose, 1978, p.204).

STRUCTURE, TECHNOLOGY AND POLITICAL CHOICE

Contingency theory is an approach in organizational analysis stressing the relationship between structure, environments and technologies. It clearly has a number of advantages over earlier attempts to link organizational configuration with performance. It has helped to establish empirically the extent to which popular stereotypes of management structure are defensible. It has demolished the idea that required organizational performance will be guaranteed by the adoption of a single set of managerial principles. It enables the relative importance of different contingencies to be evaluated within an interdependent network of circumstances, structures and performance. The business of selecting an appropriate management structure should become easier under the influence of a contingency approach.

The key term here, however, is 'selection'. Choices have to be made within organizations by key personnel. A contingency approach should not make the mistake of assuming that contingencies somehow act as the impersonal determinant of structural configurations. We should not regard organizational change as merely an intellectual and technocratic exercise, seeing the determinants of optimum organization as only having to be understood to be applied. This would lead us to ignore internal political and technical factors which make adaptation to contingencies far more than a matter of mere logistics. Organizational change should be regarded as a political process in which different groups have different vested interests in the responses that may be made to the structural imperatives of organizational contingencies (Wood, 1979).

The history of organizational adaptation in the Post Office, both as a government department and a 'hived off' public corporation, is an excellent illustration of this (see chapter 6). Evidence of how internal groups can retain autonomy over processes of managerial adaptation is further revealed by post-Fulton developments in central government departments. It had been argued by Fulton that the tasks of departments required administrative staff specialization in either financial/industrial or social policy. In response to this the civil service carried out its own internal analysis of departmental tasks and concluded that this twofold division was not practicable (Brown and Steel, 1979, p.328). The report supported 'specialization' on a departmental basis, so reinforcing the status quo as far as this aspect of departmental organization was concerned.

Government departments, like other complex organizations, are pluralistic as regards the interests which may be furthered or threatened by organizational change. Senior generalists and specialists, for example, will react rather differently to suggestions that departmental structures incorporating administrative and professional activities should be reorganized in ways which affect the distribution of responsibilities, and therefore power, within them.

The first qualification of contingency theory, then, is the need to see organizational change to a large extent as a political process. The second is, as John Child has persuasively argued, that the area of choice available to the 'dominant coalitions' within organizations extends to the context of the environment itself: 'organizational

decision makers do take positive steps to define and manipulate their
own corners of the environment' (Child, 1972, p.9). The power
structure within the organization will determine its response to its
environment. Organizations can choose to ignore, or restrain the
influence of, developments within the environment and may be able to
exercise authority over other organizations and individuals. The
Department of the Environment, for example, tries to manipulate the
local response to large physical development projects such as
motorways by restricting the public inquiry process to the question
of alternative sites rather than overall need for the proposed
development. In this, it may ally itself with major road-user
interests. Another department may influence the response of clients
and claimants to its services by the way it informs the public of
their availability. By defining 'needs' in particular ways, a
department is able to exercise a measure of control over the choice
of those eligible for its services. So there is a problem in some
versions of contingency theory as to the status of the supposedly
'given' influences on organizational design. This may even extend
to a choice of technology itself (Dawson, 1979) and possibly to the
workflows and administrative processes of central departments.

Third, the strategic choices open to organizational reformers
extend to the criteria by which performance is evaluated. If these
can be manipulated then the organizational structures needed to
achieve them are much less deterministic than contingency theory
often seems to imply. If there is substantial choice of what counts
as satisfactory performance, there will be substantial areas of
choice as to how organizational structures should be planned. In
central departments decisions about how 'output' is to be measured
affect the way work is organized in units of accountable management.
If performance is to be measured in terms of parliamentary
accountability, the equitable application of public policy and
guardianship of the public purse, the departmental structure is
bound to be hierarchical and centralized. If it places more emphasis
on efficiency, rates of return on investment and cost effectiveness
it may be necessary to delegate managerial responsibility to units
within the organization that can respond freely and flexibly to
opportunities for maximizing objectives and minimizing costs.

Fourth, although contingency theory is descriptively useful, its
normative value is less certain. There is as yet no conclusive
evidence that matching organizational design to contingencies has an
overridingly important and significant effect on performance. Other
factors than structural ones may be more important in affecting
levels of performance:

> structural design is likely to have only a limited effect upon
> the level of organizational performance achieved, even though
> the type of structure utilized may affect the quality of other
> strategic decisions because of the way it influences the
> communication of necessary information and so on. (Child, 1972,
> p.12)

This problem is complicated by the fact that performance itself is
an ambiguous concept. In most organizations, including government
departments, there will be a variety of goals, and performance in
respect of each will be multifaceted. Different parts of the
organization will be concerned with effectiveness, efficiency,

productivity, morale and adaptability (Dawson, 1979, p.61). The problem of measuring performance in government departments is particularly intractable. Measuring and costing 'output' when collective goods such as education, health and welfare are the objectives, present enormous difficulty at a vital step in the normative argument of contingency theory.

Fifth, different contingencies may have conflicting implications for organizational structure. This is particularly likely in multi-purpose government departments, especially the large ones. Here there may well be a conflict between the 'iron grid effect' of uniformity in civil service structure and the adaptation of structures to task (Hood, et al., 1979, p.34). There is certainly evidence that work in departments is organized within hierarchies that reflect the career structure of the civil service. For example, while in industry and commerce data-processing staff tend to be organized in non-hierarchical specialist and innovatory groups, in the civil service computing falls to the executive grades - 'markedly hierarchical in structure, non-specialist and originally organized to manage clerical operations. Though the attempt is made to fit these grade levels to computer work - Executive Officer programmer, HED and SED systems analyst - such arrangements are under considerable strain' (Garrett, 1972, p.86). Whether these factors impede structural adaptation and therefore improved performance is impossible to say with the present state of knowledge. Even if structures were individually responding to tasks in different units within the department someone has to decide that priority should be given to this contingency rather than, say, the demand for ministerial accountability to parliament.

Finally, it has been pointed out that performance itself may not be a totally dependent variable. There may be two-way relationships between structure, performance and organizational contingencies (Dawson, 1979). Levels of performance may precipitate changes in other organizational characteristics. As our chapter on management shows, it was certainly the case that widespread concern about the supposed failings of civil servants and their poor performance triggered off the reforms of the late 1960s and early 1970s. At a less macro level, other deficiencies in performance, such as those revealed from time to time by the investigations into allegations of maladministration by the Parliamentary Commissioner for Administration, may lead to changes in decision-making procedures, perhaps causing greater bureaucratization. Of course, this phenomenon may be claimed by contingency theorists as evidence of structures adjusting to contextual factors. If this is the case, it must again be emphasized that such adjustment requires strategic choices to be made by those in positions of power or under the influence of those able to wield sanctions successfully. Our case study of the Post Office will return to this question.

Perrow's technology variables help us to see that decision-making in government departments is a more complex phenomenon than is sometimes recognized and that organizations should not be forced on to the single dimension of routine/non-routine. The implication of this approach is that structure follows technology. This simple principle is quite devastating when applied to many of the criticisms made of management in central departments which so often advocate structure regardless of technologies and tasks. In almost every branch of management theory it is now fashionable to deny that there is one ideal solution to all organizational problems. Universal principles of organization are a thing of the past. This seems particularly sensible in the case of government departments.

A contingency approach is gradually being introduced into the study of public administration, particularly local government. This approach studies organizations in the context of their tasks as well as environment in order to contribute to the business of finding the correct structural solutions to organizational problems.

It is, however, easy to see why standardized forms of organizational structure might have developed across the range of central departments and the administrative tasks in which they are engaged. The regulative nature of much central administration, whether in relation to subordinate administrative agencies or private individuals and organizations, inevitably produces structures appropriate to routine administration according to precise rules. This is further strengthened by environmental factors, such as the need for the equitable treatment of those brought within the rules devised to implement policies, and the centralized forms of accountability, both financial and political. There is also the fact that a single department will be multifunctional and have to perform many different tasks. The pressures for standardized rather than diversified structures are bound to be strong.

In addition, those who wish to recommend alternative structures are obliged to show that they are likely to be more effective, efficient, productive and so on. In central government efficiency is something which can be defined and measured only with great difficulty and caution because of the highly intangible nature of what is 'produced'. A recent concern of managers in central departments has been to improve methods of planning in order to reveal more about the costs of undertaking different activities and the nature and quantity of what those activities achieve. The process of management in the context of central government is the subject of our next chapter.

Chapter 5

MANAGEMENT IN GOVERNMENT DEPARTMENTS

No organization can function well if it is ineffectively managed. This self-evident statement applies with equal force to organizations as varied as schools, businesses, hospitals and government departments The job of the manager can be broken down into the following component elements. First, he must establish objectives; he must determine what the targets are that the organization is trying to achieve and work out an appropriate strategy for achieving them. Second, he must devote considerable attention to the question of organizational design, establishing an effective communications system and maintaining a high degree of co-ordination. Third, he must recruit staff with relevant qualifications and motivate them to work for the attainment of organizational objectives. Finally, he must provide adequate 'feedback' or control mechanisms to enable him to check the performance of staff against targets and plans.

During the 1960s it became fashionable to suggest that government departments were ineffectively managed. A host of critics argued that the structures, personnel and working practices of government departments were unsuited to the tasks undertaken by the modern state. Such criticism received encouragement from a series of inquiries into government departments revealing an absence of clear objectives, out-of-date organizational structures, outmoded recruitment and training programmes and non-existent performance appraisal methods. Government organizations had apparently fallen behind their private sector counterparts in the use of modern management techniques.

The implication was that successful methods of management in the private sector should be imported into the public sector. This philosophy, widely known as 'managerialism', stressed the essential similarity between all organizations. In addition, it provided its adherents with a set of critical values by means of which traditional working practices within government departments could be evaluated and, hopefully, changed. In this chapter, we shall attempt to assess some of the criticisms made of government organizations during this period. Our intention is to demonstrate that, while many of them were relevant and useful in the context of the changing environment faced by many departments since the Second World War, the wholesale transfer of techniques and ideas found

valuable in one type of organization (private business) to another
(government department) may be fraught with difficulty.

What follows is an examination of the managerialist critique of
government departments. We shall trace the origins of that critique
to the widespread feelings of disappointment with the performance of
successive governments during the 1950s and attendant calls for
reform in government departments culminating in the Report of the
Fulton Committee in 1968, a thoroughgoing managerialist document.
In addition, we shall evaluate the claims of those pressing for the
adoption of working practices akin to those in private enterprise
by pointing out that the task of management within the public sector
must be conducted within a political environment. As chapter 2
revealed, a particular set of 'institutionalized values' constrains
the activities of members of government departments. Such
constraints, largely absent in private sector organizations,
constitute important limitations on any wholesale importation of
more 'businesslike' philosophies of management into government
agencies.

While organizational theory undoubtedly played a part in
supporting the adoption of managerialist views - for example, the
arguments of Fulton in favour of more flexible organizational
structures owed much to the 'discovery' of the 'organic' organization
by writers such as Burns and Stalker and Woodward - it can play a
part too in exposing certain myths and fallacies in the managerialist
case. The adoption of an organizational theory approach to government
departments will assist an understanding and evaluation of the
similarities and differences between private and public sector
organizations providing, hopefully a balanced perspective on the
salient characteristics of each.

ACTIVE GOVERNMENT, BUREAUCRACY AND CHANGE

Without doubt the most important factor encouraging the argument
that government departments should adopt the managerial practices
of private enterprise organizations, was a growing realization that
the work of government had changed considerably as a result of two
world wars and changing public attitudes and demands. Changes in
task in government departments prompted questions about changes in
methods; specifically, were the personnel, practices and organizational structures well suited to meet the demands of new functions?
Changes in task prompted too the thought that if the activities of
government in, for example, commercial and industrial fields were
becoming more like those of business concerns, principles of
management successfully utilized in private firms could advantageous-
ly be adopted in the public sector. As one of the most thoughtful
commentators on this period has suggested, the concern arose as to
whether the conventional bureaucratic practices of British public
administration were any longer 'appropriate to departments which
have acquired executive responsibilities on the scale of the
largest businesses' (Garrett, 1972, p.1).

CRITICISMS OF PERSONNEL

Acknowledgment of the increasingly important role of civil servants in the policy-making process was accompanied in the years immediately prior to the appointment of the Fulton Committee by fears that the background, education, and training of civil servants were not well-attuned to the varying demands being placed upon government. Two factors appear to account for increasing criticism of the civil service at this time: first, the realization that active government implied a shift in power from Westminster to Whitehall (from the elected politician to the appointed official); second, a series of national disappointments resulting from ineffective or miscalculated government policy. The picture emerged of a political and administrative system lacking a sense of purpose, direction and co-ordination. At the very pinnacle of the civil service structure and sharing with ministers the responsibility for important policy decisions, the Administrative Class began to bear the brunt of many adverse comments. These were that it was ill-equipped by background and education to comprehend the social, economic and scientific changes which were confronting Britain.

Two basic criticisms of top civil servants emerged in the post War years. The first was that they constituted a tightly knit elite, bound together by an exclusive social and educational background, temperamentally hostile to change and collectively determined to ensure the continuance of traditional values in public life. Such a view found expression in a celebrated broadside delivered against the civil service by the journalist Henry Fairlie in 1955. Identifying top civil servants as part of an 'establishment', he accused them of standing in the way of necessary progress and preventing the adoption of changes in the system of government.

Serious doubts about the social exclusiveness of civil servants were accompanied by misgivings about their efficiency. One of the most important charges levelled against the Administrative Class at this time was that it lacked professional competence, i.e. specialist skills relevant to management and administration in a complex society. The administrative grades were attacked for their amateur approach to the problems of government. In a widely publicized essay written in 1959 Thomas Balogh, an Oxford economist popularized this theme by accusing top civil servants of lacking technical expertise and being unversed in the modern disciplines of economics and management studies, both of which he considered directly relevant to the affairs of modern government departments (1959). This theme was taken up in a pamphlet produced by the Fabian Society (1964). This attacked selection procedures for their bias in appointing graduates with irrelevant general arts degrees, and training procedures which failed to provide instruction in appropriate relevant subjects. Containing no startlingly new revelations, its critique of the civil service was nevertheless given added weight in that it was widely believed to have been written, anonymously, by a group of highly placed members of the Administrative Class.

Questions about the amateur status of the Administrative Class were linked to doubts about the wisdom of subordinating professional (vocationally trained) officials such as scientists and engineers to generalist (lay) personnel. The subordination of specialist to administrative personnel became a salient issue in a period of increasing government involvement in technical and scientific policy. Such a system was deemed to be wildly at odds with personnel practices in industry, where the place of the specialist in top decision-making management posts was long assured. Professional groups in government repeatedly complained about the relatively disadvantaged position of the expert official. These complaints were given added force by the realization that British practice was out of step with other public services. The French civil service, it was claimed, has never sought to separate out specialist and administrative functions. French professional civil servants have long enjoyed much higher status and prestige and better career prospects than their British counterparts, playing a central role in policy formulation and high level administrative work. Commenting on this matter, Professor Brian Chapman (1963) concluded that the British civil service constituted a closed elite which had voluntarily shut its collective mind to the advantages to be gained from the acquisition and utilization of specialized knowledge of direct relevance to the running of a modern economy and society.

CRITICISMS OF PRACTICES

Criticisms of the competence of civil servants were supplemented by doubts about the methods employed in government departments to achieve their goals. Again, unfavourable comparisons were drawn between the public and private sectors. The rationality of decision-making methods was a favourite target. While industry was seen as pursuing well defined objectives, systematically choosing the most appropriate means for achieving them, departments were characterized as pursuing short-term rather than long-term ends. Reacting to the pressures of day-to-day events rather than developing a strategic view of their mission, departments were forced to resort to a disjointed and unco-ordinated decision-making process.

Planning became something of an infatuation in Britain in the 1960s. The major reason for this was, once again, economic. Britain's poor economic performance and failure to achieve growth was linked, in the view of the critics, to a failure on the part of governments to establish a clear cut set of economic targets and the appropriate administrative means to achieve them (Smith, 1979).

The call for more effective economic planning was paralleled by pressures for improvements in the planning capacity of government departments. The adoption of a planning approach in departments would, it was felt, bring several clear advantages. First, it would require civil servants to think more systematically about what they were doing. Second, it would develop in them a greater awareness of the future impact of their decisions. This was a major significance when the long-term implications of government activities were becoming more and more pronounced, for instance in the formulation and implementation of large capital-intensive projects such as nuclear power stations. Third, it would provide a useful discipline, forcing civil servants to clarify their

objectives and the options open to them for achieving them. Finally,
it would enable the adoption of a more 'synoptic' or integrated
approach to decision-making in the system as a whole. It would
thus counteract tendencies towards fragmentation and incoherence.
The adoption of planning techniques and philosophies, owing much to
outside practice in private industry, would enable departments to
'search for the best use of resources in pursuit of objectives'
(Keeling, 1972, p.32).

Two events marked the growing concern with planning. The first
was the report of the Estimates Committee of the House of Commons
in 1958. The second, was that of the Plowden Committee on the
Control of Public Expenditure in 1961. The Estimates Committee
suggested that the Treasury, the most prestigious and powerful
member of the departmental system, charged with the unique responsibility of exercising financial and administrative control over the
rest, played its role unsystematically. Instead of concentrating
on the long-term implications of departmental policy proposals, the
Treasury spent most of its time on the examination of annual
Estimates. At best, departmental policy proposals involving
expenditure were only considered for one year ahead.

Following a recommendation of the Select Committee, another
small committee under the chairmanship of Lord Plowden was set up
to review in depth the system of Treasury expenditure control.
Plowden argued that 'regular surveys should be made of public
expenditure as a whole over a period of years ahead, and in relation
to prospective resources; decisions involving substantial future
expenditure should be taken in the light of these surveys'. This
launched a series of planning reforms in departments which has
continued to the present day. It also effectively endorsed the
view that existing financial controls, while in keeping with the
traditional institutional value that expenditure should be legal
and incurred only on projects and programmes approved by parliament,
were essentially negative and out of place in a modern managerial
system concerned not only with the bureaucratic virtue to regularity
but with the entrepreneurial values of efficiency and effectiveness.
Parliamentary and Treasury control of departments' finances was
also based more on a concern with the 'inputs' of decision making
such as numbers of civil servants, desks, stationery etc., than
with its 'outputs' and the alternative uses to which resources
could be put.

Concern with the professional competence of civil service staff
at this time was reflected in Plowden's observations that the
adoption of modern planning methods within departments would have
to be accompanied by a changing conception of the role of personnel.
Instead of seeing themselves simply in the secretarial role of
offering policy advice to ministers, civil servants ought to regard
themselves as managers of human and material resources. To this
end they should be better equipped with quantitative and statistical
skills to enable them to evaluate different programmes and the costs
of alternative courses of action. They also needed human relations
skills for the effective deployment and motivation of their staff.

CRITICISMS OF ORGANIZATIONAL STRUCTURES

Here two questions concerned reformers. First, whether the pattern
of interrelationships between departments made the pursuit of
mutually compatible strategies possible. Second, whether the
internal structures of departments were best suited to changing
governmental tasks.

Acceptance of the philosophy of planning was matched by the
suspicion that the distribution of functions between departments
was haphazard, owing less to logic than to historical accident.
With the growth of 'active' government, pressures to increase the
number of departments have grown since the First World War. However,
an opposing pressure was in evidence in the 1950s, that of co-
ordinating a number of widely varying departments in the interest
of efficient administration. After 1955 a number of departmental
mergers took place. Previously separate departments were joined,
such as the Ministries of Pensions and National Insurance in 1953,
and Food and Agriculture in 1955. This trend was continued in the
1960s. In 1964, the Ministry of Defence emerged as the result of
the amalgamation of the three previously separate services
departments and part of the old Ministry of Supply. The Foreign and
Commonwealth Office was constructed out of the separate Foreign,
Commonwealth and Colonial Offices and the Ministry of Overseas
Development. In 1968, the Department of Health and Social Security
was formed out of the Departments of Health, Pensions and National
Insurance. The object of such amalgamation was clear – to obtain
greater coherence and integration in closely related policy areas,
an aim consistent with the move to greater planning.

The question of the distribution of functions was accompanied
by doubts about the internal structure of departments. In
particular, there was the problem of their characteristically
bureaucratic design. Critics pointed to the more flexible organizational patterns which they claimed to discern in outside industry.
In this, they were aided by a series of studies in the field of
organizational analysis which showed that when managers faced
changing circumstances, or were working with certain technologies,
they tended to discard bureaucratic, or 'mechanistic' organizational
structures in favour of more flexible, 'organic' alternatives. We
have referred to the work of some of these 'contingency' theorists,
for example Woodward and Perrow, in an earlier chapter. Following
a study of the Scottish electronics industry, two of these writers,
Tom Burns and G.M. Stalker (1961), concluded that mechanistic
patterns of organization were only really appropriate for handling
stable and predictable tasks. In situations of change, however,
more flexible organizational structures were needed. The conclusion
drawn was that departments, involved increasingly in highly technical
and commercial functions and facing changing values and demands,
should abandon bureaucracy in favour of a more flexible and
responsive organizational format.

THE FULTON COMMITTEE – HIGH WATER MARK OF MANAGERIALISM

In its 1964 election manifesto, 'Signposts for the Sixties', the

Labour Party declared its commitment to a thoroughgoing policy of
national renewal based on a new scientific and technological
revolution. This entailed major reforms in the system of government,
including the civil service. Complaints of amateurism continued and
the introduction of outside experts and the development of more
professional skills were demanded. The Estimates Committee produced
a report on the civil service in 1965 which accused it of having an
image out of keeping with the times. Its Administrative Class was
again criticized for drawing its members from a relatively closed
and highly privileged section of British society. It denied itself
the talents of applicants from non-Oxbridge universities. The
report concluded with a call for the appointment of a Royal Commission
to inquire into the structure and working of the civil service
(Select Committee on Estimates, 1965). The Prime Minister, Harold
Wilson, responded by setting up the Fulton Committee. This would
'examine the structure, recruitment and management, including
training of the ... civil service and make recommendations'. In
the course of a lengthy analysis, the committee sponsored wide-
ranging reviews of the methods employed in the conduct of government
business and the departmental structures within which they were
used. Fundamental criticisms were made of most aspects of civil
service work.

The report of the committee, published in 1968, contained a
shattering indictment of the civil service and the departmental
organization which it staffed. It declared boldly that the 'Civil
Service today is still fundamentally the product of the nineteenth
century .... The tasks it faces are those of the second half of the
twentieth century. This is what we have found; it is what we seek
to remedy' (Fulton Committee, 1968, para. 1).

AN IMPORTANT LEGACY OF THE PAST

The birth date of the modern civil service was 1853. Prior to that
time there was no single unified service in this country. Civil
servants were neither recruited nor trained by one single agency of
government; instead, each department recruited its permanent
officials on the basis of personal favouritism. Such a 'spoils' or
patronage system was hardly conducive to efficiency. General public
dissatisfaction with a corrupt appointments system, and the resulting
inefficiency to which it gave rise, came to a head during the Crimean
War when the administrative failures of civil servants (for instance,
supplying the troops with the incorrect calibre of ammunition for
their guns) became visible for all to see. The Northcote-Trevelyan
reforms established that the service should be organized around
four key principles. First, recruitment would no longer be based
on favouritism and nepotism, but would be conducted by means of
open, competitive examinations. Second, a clear distinction would
be drawn between individuals deemed suitable for 'superior' or
'intellectual' positions, and those who would occupy 'lower class'
or 'mechanical' positions. Third, the service would be unified by
the establishment of a uniform grading and salary structure applying
across all departments. This would enable civil servants to be
transferred freely between departments without loss of salary or

status. Finally, promotion would be awarded primarily on the grounds
of demonstrated merit rather than by automatic seniority. All of
these principles are fundamental characteristics of a bureaucratic
form of organization. It is imperative not to lose sight of the
benefits of such organization. The managerialist critique exemplified
in Fulton can be criticized for precisely this failing.

THE FULTON EXERCISE

Fulton made six major criticisms. First, it returned to the
familiar criticism of amateurism, stating that the policy of appointing
generalists to top level posts was 'a cult obsolete at all levels and
in all parts of the Service.' In addition, the practice of constantly
moving civil servants between jobs was damaging. It effectively
prevented them from acquiring detailed knowledge and expertise in
depth of important areas of work.
    Second, the system of classes in the service was seriously
impeding its work. It was the single most important factor contributing to bureaucratic rigidity. Its major defect was its rigid
compartmentalism. It prejudiced the promotion prospects of able
individuals and discouraged initiative.
    Third, members of specialist classes were denied opportunities
in the existing system and prevented from getting access to top
level decision-making posts. Fourth, the Administrative Class
retained an outmoded conception of their own role, seeing themselves
primarily as the confidantes and advisers of ministers, giving
inadequate attention to the job of 'organisation, directing staff,
planning the progress of work, setting standards of attainment and
measuring results, reviewing procedures and quantifying different
courses of action'.
    Fifth, the service was too insulated from the outside community.
In the first place, it was sealed off from important developments
in industry and the universities. New ideas about management in
organizations developed both by academics and practitioners in
industry failed to percolate through. In the second place, the
social backgrounds and educational experiences of new entrants
remained stubbornly narrow and exclusive. Finally, the report
concluded that training and personnel management, generally
considered as having increasing importance in industry, were
'insufficiently purposive and (not) properly conceived'.
    In place of a highly fragmented class structure, it recommended
the adoption of a 'continuous grading system' within a series of
major occupational groupings. Within each grouping, existing
rigid demarcations between grades would be abolished. In addition,
posts within the revised system would be subject to a process of
rigorous job evaluation, with the duties and performance of
individuals being subjected to a process of analysis and measurement.
No posts would be the automatic preserve of one particular group.
To meet the criticism of amateurism, Fulton proposed that administrative jobs within the service should be grouped into those broadly
concerned with economic and financial matters and those involving
social questions such as education, social security and industrial
relations. Administrators should specialize in one of these areas

and should develop not only general administrative abilities as in
the past, but acquire, too, appropriate specialist qualifications
and experience in subjects such as business administration, finance
and economics. In addition, greater access would be given to
professional groups to engage in general administrative work should
they show a particular aptitude for it.

General efficiency would be further enhanced by the adoption of
up-to-date management control systems and more effective planning
mechanisms. Here they offered some radical new approaches. First,
they concluded that efficiency within large organizations depends
to a considerable degree on a structure which permits a clear
definition of authority and responsibility for which individuals
could be held directly accountable. The success of such a structure
would depend on the willing delegation of responsibility to
individuals at relatively low levels in the hierarchy. Two factors
tended to militate against such delegation. The system of
ministerial and parliamentary responsibility tended to reinforce
centralizing tendencies within the organization. Far from
encouraging the exercise of greater initiative at lower levels,
it encouraged the upward referral of decisions to higher authority
for prior authorization. In addition, the relatively 'tall'
hierarchy of most departments tended to diffuse responsibility
rather than concentrating it.

Impressed by the adoption in industry of 'management by objectives'
a system of control in which the manager and his subordinates jointly
agree a set of targets which they are given adequate resources
(finance, personnel, etc.) to meet, and 'corporate planning' whereby
the activities and objectives of each part of the organization are
combined together in a comprehensive overall strategy, the committee
pressed for the adoption of 'accountable and efficient' management.
As we have seen in chapter 4 this involves the establishment of
accountable units in which output can be measured against costs or
other criteria and where individuals can be held personally
responsible for performance. Such a recommendation has fundamental
implications for the traditional hierarchical structure of
departments. Accountable management requires the adoption of a
'flatter', more organic, form of organization if it is to be
successful. It might even be necessary to 'hive off' certain
functions altogether and re-locate them in semi-autonomous agencies
with a much greater degree of freedom from detailed ministerial and
parliamentary control.

The second radical departure envisaged in the report was the
establishment at the highest levels within departments of 'policy
planning' units. The necessity of advising ministers and briefing
them on day-to-day matters precluded officials from engaging in the
very necessary task of looking to the long-term implications of
policy. To assist in the preparation of long-term plans it was
recommended that a Senior Policy Adviser should be appointed in
each department at the level of the permanent secretary. He would
be the head of the policy planning unit.

Other recommendations included the establishment of a Civil
Service Department to take over Treasury responsibility for
supervising the work of the civil service and to encourage the
development of a 'new style of management' within it. A Civil

Service College would be established to improve the general training
of officials and a series of management services units (another idea
derived from industrial practice) would be located in the departments
to keep constant vigilance over working practices and methods and
carry out regular efficiency audits. Finally, the committee suggested
the recruitment of 'temporary' civil servants employed on a short-term
basis to bring in fresh thinking and new ideas from industry and the
universities.

THE IMPLEMENTATION OF 'MANAGERIALISM'

The strength of the managerialist philosophy may be seen from a number
of reforms which it spawned. Between 1961 and 1970 when a newly
elected Conservative government published a White Paper re-affirming
the commitment to a 'new style' of management in public sector
organizations, many important changes took place owing much to
'managerialism'.
   A number of changes pre-dated Fulton and followed Plowden. The
single most important of these was the development of a new system of
public expenditure surveying designed to relate departmental
programmes and targets (ends) to the resources (means) available
over a five-year planning period. A small high-powered committee,
the Public Expenditure Survey Committee, comprising the principal
finance officers of the major spending departments, was given the
task of examining the surveys drawn up each May in consultations
between the Treasury and the individual departments. It reported
to the Cabinet. These surveys deal with a period of up to five
years ahead and are designed to indicate where existing policies
are leading in terms of public expenditure. Since 1969, the Public
Expenditure Survey has been published by the government in the form
of a White Paper.
   Major advantages claimed for PESC, as the system of five-year
forecasting came to be known, were many. First, it would provide
the Treasury, as principal finance ministry, with a more effective
system of allocating resources to departments on a medium and long-
term basis. Second, it would force ministers and civil servants to
examine not only the day-to-day implications of policy proposals
but their likely future effects. Third, it would require them to
adopt a programmatic perspective on the work of their departments,
viewing their objectives and related expenditures not in isolation
but in relation to those of other departments. It would thus
encourage co-ordination of government policy. Fourth, it would
allow more effective external assessment of the activities of
government departments, essential in a democratic political system,
by enabling more effective parliamentary scrutiny of the likely
future implications of departmental programmes as well as their
past failures and successes. Parliament would thus be able to
perform a much more effective role as the nation's financial
watchdog.
   In summary, the PESC system provided a more rational form of
expenditure appraisal than that previously in existence. Designed
to permit more effective understanding of the likely expenditure
consequences of current policies, it encouraged a greater commitment

in departments to planning, allowed for the establishment of
priorities for the government as a whole and accorded a much more
positive role to parliament in discussion, analysis and criticism
of government policy and related expenditure proposals. Following
criticisms of its Select Committee on Procedure, the House of
Commons replaced its Estimates Committee (its traditional instrument
of expenditure appraisal) with a new Select Committee on Expenditure
in 1969. This, it was hoped, would enable the legislature more
positively to assess the efficiency with which departments set and
realized their objectives.

Other important reforms designed to improve planning capability
accompanied the adoption of PESC. In 1962, following a recommendation
of the Plowden Committee, the Treasury was subjected to an important
internal reorganization, designed to enable it to carry out its work
of expenditure appraisal more effectively while at the same time
providing the departments with the best up-to-date advice on
questions of management and organization. This reorganization was
taken a stage further in 1964, when the responsibilities of the
Treasury for general management of the economy were transferred to
a new Department of Economic Affairs. In 1970, the new Conservative
Prime Minister, Edward Heath, established a Central Policy Review
Staff (CPRS), also known as a 'central capability unit' or 'think
tank'. This unit, utilizing the talents of not only permanent
civil servants, but also highly qualified outsiders, was designed
to act as a monitoring agency at the apex of the government machine.
In this role it serviced the Cabinet, providing ministers with
detailed analyses of important problems and keeping a close watch
on the overall strategy of governments. Since its inception, the
CPRS has examined, amongst other things, the likely effects of
government decision-making in high technology projects such as
Concorde and in economic matters such as energy policy and regional
policy. In 1973 an important refinement was added to the PESC
system in the shape of Programme Analysis and Review (PAR). This
innovation took the form of a series of reviews of key areas of
departmental policy. It was intended to complement PESC, provide
ministers with detailed analyses of the effectiveness of current
departmental programmes, and review the different means available
for achieving a set objective.

The above reforms constituted an attempt to improve the methods
employed in government departments to achieve their goals. Closely
related to them were a series of reforms designed to improve
personnel management - the recruitment, training, motivation and
deployment of staff. Following Fulton's recommendation that the
existing class structure should be rationalized, efforts were made
to replace it with a new grading system designed to achieve greater
flexibility, improve general promotion prospects by removing
previously impermeable and artificial barriers to individual
advancement and make better and more fairer use of the abilities
of professional officers.

To remove vertical barriers to upward progression, the existing
class divisions in the service were relinquished in a three-stage
exercise. In January 1971, the general classes, Administrative,
Executive and Clerical, were amalgamated to form the Administration
Group. This was followed in September of that year by a merging of

the scientific classes to form the Science Group. The exercise was completed in 1972 with the creation of the Professional and Technology Group to replace a miscellany of 'works' classes including engineers and draughtsmen. To encourage better unification of general and specialist officials within the revised structure, a unified grading system was adopted for posts at the very highest level (under-secretaries and above). It was hoped that senior positions within departments would no longer remain the monopoly of the generalist classes. Ultimately, all posts from the top to the bottom of the system would be opened up in this way.

Changes in the class structure of the civil service were accompanied by important reforms in its central management. A Civil Service Department was established in 1968 to oversee the recruitment functions of the Civil Service Commission and take over the Treasury's tasks in respect to pay and management. Two basic advantages were claimed for the new arrangement. First, responsibilities for recruitment, selection, training and career development could be integrated better under the direction of one ministry. Second, such unification would also enable better dissemination of information to departments on the use of modern management techniques and permit a more systematic oversight of organization and management within them.

The establishment of CSD marked an increasing concern with the principles upon which senior level recruitment and training were conducted in the service. The Method I system of recruitment, which presupposed that the civil service should look for entrants with both high quality and the widest possible general education, was abandoned in favour of Method II, which tested not only the candidates' general intellectual ability but also attempted through an extended interview programme to assess their potentialities for leadership and basic management skills 'directly bearing upon official business'.

Concern with recruitment procedures was linked to important advances in training. Acknowledgment of Plowden's point that civil servants should be trained in management skills was provided in the establishment of a Centre for Administrative Studies in 1963. All new entrants to the Administrative Class (assistant principals) were given a fourteen-week crash course in economic and statistical techniques. Reviewing this scheme, a Treasury working party concluded that it was too short to be useful and recommended that general training schemes should be extended. Fulton's proposal for the establishment of a Civil Service College was a direct expression of this aim. Since 1970, this College has provided general managerial training to new recruits - generalists and specialists - and for senior members of the unified structure at the apex of the service. An interesting development was the introduction in 1972 of a training course in general administrative skills for high level professional officers. Known as the 'Senior Professional Administrative Training Scheme' (SPATS) its intention was to equip them for their new role as co-equal partners with the Administration Group on top level policy-making and administrative posts.

Closely associated with reforms in methods and personnel management were changes in organizational structure. Here two basic themes were pursued, unification and decentralization. Both were

revealed in the 1970 White Paper. The trend towards departmental
amalgamations which had been proceeding during the 1960s was taken
a stage further in this document which argued that existing
departmental boundaries should be re-drawn in many cases 'to
improve the framework within which public policy is formulated by
matching the field of responsibility of government departments to
coherent fields of policy and administration'. Thus departmental
amalgamation would permit the closer co-ordination of related
functions. In practice, this meant grouping functions together in
giant departments (for example, DoE and DTI) to create areas of
unified policy.

Linked to the attempt to effect better co-ordination between
departments went an important effort to introduce new forms of
organizational control within them. This was in keeping with
Fulton's recommendation that bureaucratic accountability to external
agencies such as parliament which stress the importance of equity
and legality, should, wherever possible, be replaced by managerial
accountability. This would place less emphasis on hierarchical
authority than on objectives, related performance standards and
efficiency.

Finally, two related structural reforms deserve brief mention.
The trend we noted in chapter 3 for the abandonment of the principle
of locating specialists and generalists in parallel hierarchies and
their assimilation into unified hierarchies has proceeded still
further after Fulton. The Ministry of Public Building and Works,
for example, reformed its hierarchical structure in this way in
1969 so that specialists would be involved more closely with
generalists in the formulation of departmental policy - a practice
which has been incorporated into the 'giant' departments set up
after 1970. Similarly, Fulton's recommendation for the establishment
of planning units has been implemented in many departments.

MANAGERIALISM, BUREAUCRACY AND ORGANIZATIONAL ANALYSIS

An organizational theory perspective demonstrates that the strengths
of the managerialist approach outlined above have been accompanied
by a serious weakness. This is the dubious assumption that
techniques and practices in widespread use in the private sector
can be beneficially adopted in the public.

For many years it was customary to regard the tasks and working
practices of public and private sector organizations as being
essentially different (see chapter 1). In the first place, their
goals were seen as dissimilar. While the private entrepreneur
existed to sell goods for a profit, stimulate demand for his
products and pursue his own, narrow sectional interest, the public
administrator was charged with the integrative task of pursuing
the national or public interest. Differences in task were related
to differences in environment. Whereas the private owner occupied
a market environment stressing the values of risk taking and
competition, the public official was forced to operate in a
political environment stressing caution and public accountability
to ministers and parliament. Differences in organizational
practices were also apparent. While the private entrepreneur was

free to experiment with flexible, organic organizational designs, the requirements of public accountability imposed a monolithic bureaucratic structure on all parts of the public sector. Finally, differences in performance tests distinguished public and private organizations. Whereas the private firm could adopt reasonably straightforward tests of efficiency, measuring economic return against cost, efficiency was only one of a range of values which the public official had to adopt. Of no less importance, though admittedly much more difficult to measure, were those of legality, consistency and equity. In his dealings with both ministers and public the civil servant was enjoined to act at all times with proper respect for fairness and impartiality. He had to act as an honest broker in settling competing claims on public resources.

Several factors served to erode this polarized model of public and private organizations. Early writers on administration and management insisted that in all organizations, regardless of type, certain 'principles' of management could be applied. Taking their cue from the French writer, Henry Fayol (1949) they sought to demonstrate not the uniqueness of organizations, but their inherent similarity. What worked well in private industry would work equally well in the public sector. In addition, the extension of government activities into commercial and technical areas previously the province of private enterprise rendered the acquisition of management skills no less relevant in government departments. Linked to this was the erosion of the boundaries between public and private organizations. The development of the so-called 'mixed' economy since the Second World War has produced a closer partnership between private industry and government, especially in the management of large-scale technological projects (Concorde is a case in point). One effect of this is that civil servants have been forced to consider their role as more like that of the manager in private industry. Another is that influential 'outsiders' have lately been employed as temporary civil servants bringing into departments up-to-date management ideas and concepts.

The result of these and related trends is that arguments have surfaced calling for the replacement of the polarized view of public and private organizations by a unified model stressing not the differences, but the similarities between them. The managerialist case rests on the adoption of such a unified model. One key assumption of this model is that the goals of both sets of organizations have become more alike. Another is that the environmental values surrounding departments have changed; the criterion of efficiency, for example, has eroded more 'traditional' expectations such as accountability and equity. (We saw in earlier chapters how the key value of anonymity has been modified, as in the Vehicle and General case.)   This has led to the general assumption that as the structural requirements of departments have altered, their bureaucratic organizational forms should be replaced with the organic alternative so much in favour in the private sector.

The single most important contribution which contemporary organizational analysis has made to this debate is the conclusive demonstration that neither the polarized (or divergent) view of public and private organizations nor the unified (or convergent)

view does sufficient justice to the complexity of both public and
private organizations. Contingency analysis, by demonstrating that
all organizations regardless of their public or private characteristics vary in relation to their size, technology and environment, has
shown that variations between the broad categories of public and
private organizations are of less significance than variations
within them. The adoption of a mixed model directs our attention
to the fact that while some organizations in both sectors require
organic methods of operation others need to retain bureaucratic
forms. This observation is of considerable help in exposing faulty
logic, fallacies and hidden values in the managerialist position.

Comparison and the related activity of classification are
essential tools in the study of organizations. They represent the
first steps towards theoretical and practical understanding of
their important characteristics. We have suggested that the
managerialist critique of departments was based on a comparison
between their supposedly bureaucratic structures and working
practices and the more flexible organic practices of private
industry. However, such a comparison was subject to an important
logical flaw. It failed to draw sufficient attention to the
miscellaneous character of organizations, both public and private.
Organizational research has revealed that bureaucratic structures
and practices remain, as Max Weber noted long ago, highly effective
methods for achieving tasks in certain circumstances. The work of
Woodward, Burns and Stalker and Perrow has demonstrated that while
organizations operating within an unpredictable environment or
with a non-routine technology might require a flexible, organic
structure, for those operating in stable circumstances and with
predictable technologies, bureaucracy remains a potent force for
rationality and sound management. The implication of this argument
is that while it is reasonable to assume (as the managerialists
did) that many organizations in the public sector might benefit
from more flexible forms of organization to cope with the changing
tasks of government, it is by no means certain that all of them
would. The work of many departments remains stubbornly routine
and predictable. While government research establishments, for
example, may be adaptive, constantly innovating and dealing with
new and exciting tasks, the work of many departments is executive
and repetitive in character, for example, settling claims for
welfare and pension payments according to set rules and formulae
(see chapter 4). While the first may require the adoption of a
more organic framework of organization, it is less clear that a
bureaucratic form of organization is unsuited to the work of the
second. The force of this point is brought home by consideration
of the fact that in private organizations operating within
predictable and routine situations, bureaucracy remains the preferred
form of organization.

Contemporary organizational analysis has also done much to
explode the fallacy that departments are inevitably inefficient in
comparison with private organizations. Managerialist critics have
repeatedly catalogued their supposed failings. First, they are
vulnerable to 'Gresham's Law' (as we suggested in chapter 3).
Concern with day-to-day problems displaces planning and long-term
decision-making. Second, they are inevitably slow and cumbersome

placing excessive reliance on detailed record keeping and consistency rather than flexibility. Third, they are over-cautious. They place more value on the somewhat negative goal of 'mistake avoidance' rather than the positive one of 'risk-taking' (Keeling, 1972). Fourth, they are over-centralized. The stress on caution and consistency reinforces a process of upward referral of decision-making to the highest echelons in the organization. Junior officials are constantly encouraged to refer difficult decisions to their superiors rather than acting on their own initiative. Finally, detailed rules and the adoption of a rigidly hierarchical form of organization de-motivate the individual member of the bureaucracy. Feeling himself an isolated cog in the machine, he experiences a sense of alienation and is thereby discouraged from giving his best efforts to the pursuit of organizational goals. Bureaucracy, as some critics have remarked, is an unfit place for intelligent adults to work in.

Academic analysis in recent years has revealed that, assuming the above list of weaknesses of bureaucracy to be accurate, they are quite as typical of large organizations in the private sector as in the public. Examination of the activities of private sector managers shows that they, too, frequently devote more attention to short-run rather than long-term goals (Stewart, 1967). Just as the work of top decision-makers within the civil service is subject to the encroachments of day-to-day problems, so too is the activity of managers affected by the 'despotism of the present'; their long-term planning activities are typically displaced by constant interruption. In addition, as Drucker has shown (1968), the widely accepted image of the manager as constantly innovating and taking risks in the interests of profit maximization ought, realistically, to be abandoned. Often he seeks the sanctuary of mistake avoidance strategies rather than engage in risky and speculative commercial ventures. The history of the past twenty years is littered with a host of official reports and academic and journalistic comments (strangely ignored by the managerialist critics of departments) of flaccid and weak-willed management in the private sector. These have pointed to its poor record of capital investment in new plant and machinery and its disappointing performance compared with its peers abroad. The Finniston Report, recently published and the last in a long line of similar inquiries, has commented adversely on the under-utilization of engineering and professional skills in private management. Criticism of the dominance of 'lay' management at the top levels of British industry has become a familiar refrain. Similarly, the investigation of company practices in many large organizations has shown that centralization of decision-making, an assumed fault of departments, is a preferred organizational strategy in some successful and efficient companies. Marks and Spencer is a case in point. Finally, criticisms of the authoritarian style of management in government organizations has been paralleled in the private sector. Investigations of personnel practices in outside industry have frequently alluded to the reluctance of management to utilize modern motivational devices such as 'management by objectives' in favour of a simpler approach based on the traditional assumption that the effective use of staff talents depends less on consultation and agreement (the 'Theory Y' approach) than on direction and the imposition of orders ('Theory X'). Alienation of staff is regarded as the inevitable outcome.

Besides pointing to shared problems between the public and private
sectors, current academic writing on organization has gone some way
to disenfranchise dominant simplistic views of the bureaucratic
organization. Again, important lessons may be drawn from this
exercise. For many years bureaucracy has been regarded in almost
wholly negative terms. From the writings of Balzac and Orwell to
the views of the so-called 'man in the stree', the term bureaucracy
has summoned up an image of the socially undesirable. Such views
were supported by the work of some organizational writers who argued
that bureaucratic organizations display a set of dysfunctions.
Robert Merton (1940), for example, suggested that bureaucratic
officials typically display ritualistic behaviour, interpreting
rules in a strict and unbending manner even at the cost of providing
inadequate service to their clients. Means become more important
than ends (see chapter 3). Michel Crozier (1964), studying the
working of French government agencies concluded that they were
ponderous and incapable of innovation. More recently, however,
more hopeful messages have emerged from organizational analysis.
Reflecting on the literature on bureaucracy, Perrow has provided a
more optimistic view of such organizations (1972). He has shown
that hierarchy and rules, far from being impediments to organizational goal attainment, are, rather, necessary conditions for its
success. The complete absence of rules and settled procedures
could easily produce corruption and incompetence - as the case of
the pre-Northcote-Trevelyan civil service clearly demonstrated
(see p. 92). Other important criticisms of the negative or
'perjorative' view of bureaucracy have pointed out that the very
conditions of change which bureaucracy is seen as being incapable
of handling have often been brought about by those very organizations in the first place. Similarly, doubt has been cast on the
pessimistic view that individuals find working conditions in
bureaucracy unacceptable. Warren Bennis, a foremost critic of
the alienating effects of bureaucratic organizations in recent
years, has queried his earlier expressed view that we should
abandon bureaucracy. He has insisted that for many individuals it
provides certainty and stability in a changing world. Far from
de-motivating him, it may provide him with the security necessary
for the liberation of his productive drives (1970). The central
lesson of such views is that we must not abandon bureaucratic
principles without reminding ourselves that certain important
costs may follow. The failure of managerialist critics of
departments to acknowledge such views indicates that they may be
engaged less in an objective analysis of bureaucracy than in a
partisan and somewhat doctrinaire approach to the whole problem.
The most obvious consequences of such a position is that they
overstress the failures of bureaucracy while undervaluing its not
inconsiderable successes.

Finally, organizational theory writings remind us that changing
organizations is no easy task. Acknowledgment of the difficulties
involved in re-casting organizations has led to the emergence
within the field of organizational analysis of a sub-branch of the
discipline known as 'organizational-development' (OD). The central
tenet of this body of writing is that the goal of change may be
rendered unattainable if insufficient attention is devoted to the

methods adopted for bringing it about. Recognition of the importance
of this often overlooked fact has sprung from the realization that if
change is forced on a reluctant staff, it may actively conspire to
resist it (see chapter 3). Weight has been given to this view by
the development of a perspective in the analytical literature which
no longer sees organizations as machines in which everybody conforms
with the wishes of management, but as 'systems of negotiated order'
in which individuals and groups bargain with their conformity and
loyalty in return for satisfactory conditions of employment. Linked
to this is the understanding that organizations enshrine sets of
values. Groups may have an investment in the status quo – whether
it be bureaucratic or organic. Any attempt deliberately to alter
prevailing organizational values, for example equity, consistency,
etc., may be perceived as a threat by key sets of participants who
may possess the resources to block it or render it inoperative.

FULTON: AN ASSESSMENT

An examination of the Fulton Report in the light of organizational
analysis findings throws into relief its strengths and weaknesses.
The Report served as a useful vehicle for focusing the managerialist
discontents then current and stimulated a valuable debate on the
current state of public administration. Its membership included
people with wide experience of work in both the public and private
sectors. It sponsored important research into departments through
the medium of a Management Consultancy Group which examined blocks
of work performed by civil servants and subjected them to detailed
and careful critical analysis.
    However, praise for the work of the committee must be tempered
by recognition of its important weaknesses. First, it succumbed
to the dominant prejudice of the times that the civil service and
the system of departments were 'locked into their past' and were
uniquely unfitted to the tasks of a modern technological age.
This is evident from its opening paragraph (already quoted).
Analysis of the process of goal diffusion and multiplication in
British government during this century (see chapter 3) should alert
us to difficulties in this position. It represented a simplistic
and somewhat erroneous picture of the responsiveness of departments
to change. As we have seen, experiments with departmental mergers,
the adoption of planning systems and the merging of hierarchies –
all seen as essential requirements of a flexible administrative
structure – anticipated Fulton. In addition, new methods of
recruitment and training were utilized in response to shifting
needs. In the next chapter we shall provide evidence for our
assertion by examination of the work of the Post Office. This will
show that recognition of the merits of more organic patterns of
organization has been a feature of departmental thinking and
administrative practice for many years. Similarly, a jaundiced
eye should be cast over Fulton's implicit assumption that departments
have traditionally fallen behind industry in the adoption of up-to-
date management techniques. Historical analysis shows that
departments have often spearheaded the adoption of new techniques.
Organization and methods and operational research were pioneered in

government, for example, during the Second World War and later diffused to the private sector. A concern with planning was a strong feature of central administration in the years immediately following the cessation of hostilities in 1945 (long before the 'discovery' of planning in many companies).

The second problem revealed in Fulton is a naive understanding of the peculiar nature of the environment within which public organizations operate. Viewing the question of reform in departments as a technical problem which required a technical solution (the adoption of 'rational' structures and procedures) it underemphasized important constitutional and political factors influencing the work of civil servants. This lent an element of redundancy to its diagnoses and remedies for the problems it perceived. To be fair, Fulton was hamstrung on this point by its terms of reference, which prevented it from asking fundamental questions about the continued usefulness of important constitutional doctrines, such as ministerial accountability. Thus diverted, it directed its attention to the less sensitive areas of internal management structures and practices. However, as modern organizational theory quite clearly demonstrates, the shape, methods and fates of organizations are inextricably linked to their external environments. Failure to appreciate this point can prejudice attempts to effect important internal changes. Fulton's criticisms of the work of the Administrative Class illustrates this point. Here the committee once again bowed to popular prejudice and characterized Administrative Class officials not as 'generalists' - a term indicating an ability to take a wide-ranging view of the work of departments, but as 'amateurs' (a term used as an epithet connoting inefficiency). Fulton's attack on the Administrative Class was both unfair and inaccurate. It failed to accord due recognition to the fact that generalist civil servants frequently developed a high level of expertise and specialized knowledge of the work of particular departments (a point recently made by Sir Leo Pliatzky, an ex-Treasury permanent secretary who has pointed out that civil servants are not moved around with as much frequency as some critics claim). In setting great store on the need for improving the managerial role of civil servants, it also downplayed the importance of their political role as policy influentials, giving advice to ministers. As Eric Hobsbawm, one of its leading critics suggested, the committee incorrectly identified generalists with amateurs and obscured the important fact that the former had a legitimate place in any political/administrative system. As R.G.S. Brown (1979) has claimed, the generalist is well equipped to deal with the following tasks (of greater importance in government than private organizations). First, as a facilitator, ensuring that political ideas are properly processed and implemented. Second, as a mediator, processing specialist advice for the minister, and third, as an arbiter, reconciling both competing priorities and claims on resources.

Fulton's failure to acknowledge the impact of the political environment on departments is graphically illustrated, too, in its proposals for the reform of departmental structure. It quite evidently embraced the fashionable orthodoxy that more organic principles of organization should be adopted. In this, it was supported by its Management Consultancy Group. However, where this group had pointed to political limitations on the implementation of organic practices, the Report tended to ignore them. Its assumption that the key 'carrier' of decentralization - accountable management - could be widely adopted was based on an insufficient appreciation of the fact that political factors constituted a strong force for its antithesis, centralization. It also appeared to adopt a 'one best way' approach to the problems of organization, an approach long since abandoned by thoughtful analysts. It failed to pay due attention to the fact that, while organic principles of organizations were well suited to certain departments and parts of departments, bureaucratic structures had continuing relevance for others (see chapter 4).

Finally, the document was politically naive in failing to appreciate the significance of the point that the success of organizational change depends, to a considerable extent, on the level of skill employed by the 'change agent' in persuading people affected by it of its importance and necessity. It is a sad fact that Fulton's failure to acknowledge the degree to which change had occurred within departments in response to environmental pressure alienated those very groups within them upon whom it had to depend for the success of its proposals - civil servants.

REFORM AND CHANGE - LIMITS TO MANAGERIALISM

We conclude this chapter by pointing to some of the situational constraints on the adoption of the 'managerialist manifesto' contained in Fulton. Here again, organizational analysis is of service. In the first place, by drawing attention to the different environments within which organizations operate, it throws considerable doubt on the relevance of transferring, wholesale, methods and working practices from private to public organizations. It also offers the warning that alterations or reforms in the structures and procedures of departments, like other organizations, may not constitute radical change in their methods of operation. The implementation of change may be muted by events unforeseen by its proponents or by practical difficulties. Similarly, it may be eroded by groups within organizations perceiving it as a threat to existing practices in whose continuance they have a stake. The cosmetic may triumph over the substantive.

Despite the fact that many important traditional values surrounding the work of departments have changed over the years, it remains broadly true that the environment of such organizations is distinct from that of their private sector counterparts. Decision-making within departments takes place within a political system concerned with the public interest. Constrained by the need to act fairly and equitably as regards different groups and sectors, the civil servant cannot apply simple tests of efficiency in isolation from other considerations. In taking account of the national interest he must pay due attention to the equally important values of consistency, impartiality, fairness and equity. As a result, the importation of management techniques from outside industry becomes problematical. Uncritical adoption of devices such

as accountable management, for example, which stresses the virtues
of measuring performance and results in quantitative terms, may
divert attention away from unquantifiable, but none the less
important, aspects of administrative work, thus producing goal
displacement. Of major significance, too, is the fact that
departments frequently experience changes of political leadership
and consequent changes in policy (see chapter 3). Settled, long-
term planning is, as a consequence, difficult. Finally, organizational
continuity may be disrupted by political factors. In 1969, for
example, the Department of Economic Affairs was disbanded, not
because it had completed its task as a planning agency, but because
it had become a nuisance and embarrassment to Treasury ministers
(and officials). In the same year Harold Wilson, planning to sack
four of his Cabinet colleagues, proposed to camouflage the move
under what Richard Crossman has called a 'big piece of departmental
reconstruction'. Such an incident indicates that matters of
political expediency may take precedence over those of administrative
rationality.

Political considerations affect not only the relevance of private
sector techniques but their successful implementation. The greatest
single obstacle to the successful implementation of accountable
management and hiving off - two of Fulton's most important reform
proposals - has been that of public accountability. While Fulton
undoubtedly stimulated a drive for greater delegation of authority
in departments, real practical constraints remain on the extension
of these schemes. Ministerial responsibility continues to impose
inexorable pressures for centralization. Accountable management
and hiving off are both premised on the decentralization of
responsibility and resources to line management. Yet it is
inevitable that operating constraints on the freedom of civil
servants in the field of resource management are more severe than
in industry. It is extremely unlikely that relatively junior civil
servants will be provided with the power to make discretionary
awards to their subordinates for good performance, for example, to
the extent practicable in industry. Salaries, increments and
promotion questions remain the responsibility of the Civil Service
Department rather than the prerogative of individual departments.
Similarly, greater authority and responsibility cannot be delegated
to individual civil servants without bringing about fundamental
changes in the relationships between the civil service and parliament.
The principle of accountable management means that both ministers
and parliamentarians would normally refrain from detailed
interference with the work of civil servants acting within a sphere
of delegated authority. Neither has so far been willing to show
this degree of self-restraint. Hiving off, too, has proved
relatively unpopular for similar reasons. The establishment of
functions previously located in departments in semi-autonomous
agencies has been widely seen as a threat to the unity of the
departmental system. The drive for unification was, as we have
seen, one of the key goals of the managerialist reform proposals.

Closely linked to political constraints on change are economic
ones. Commentators have pointed out that economic inflation in
Britain in the 1970s has deflected concern with long-term planning
(based on the assumption of increasing economic resources) into a

concern with cutting back levels of departmental expenditure. Such a process has rendered the PESC and PAR system, to an extent, inoperable. Similarly, the adoption of pay restraint policies on the part of successive governments has prevented the extension of the open grading structure in the civil service below assistant secretary level.

One of the most important recent contributions of organizational analysis lies in pointing out that organizational change may be subject to important internal constraints. The introduction of change into an organization is rendered complicated by virtue of the fact that it is not simply a machine but a system of negotiated order. As we saw in chapter 3, conflict may take place within an organization over its goals. This is particularly evident when periods of change occur. They may disturb the existing social equilibrium of an organization, based as it is on a delicate balance of competing interests. Those perceiving themselves disadvantaged by change will mobilize their resources and power to prevent it or mitigate its effects. Former Administrative Class officials are in a particularly powerful position in this respect. Since the publication of Fulton, frequent complaints have been made that they have acted to prevent the full-blown adoption of some of the Report's recommendations. In the first place it is claimed that they have mobilized bias against the introduction of certain reforms. They have successfully prevented the appointment of senior policy advisers in departments, for example, on the grounds that they would challenge the authority of permanent secretaries. A more subtle form of power is what R.G.S. Brown has called 'selective inattention'. Like Nelson, civil servants have proved adept at turning a blind eye to certain reforms. It seems hardly accidental that relatively few professionals have been admitted to posts in the open structure at the top of the service, nor that the so-called 'classless' system seems to be such in name only - the generalist administrator is still pre-eminent. In the pluralistic world within organizations, conflict will arise between groups over the distribution of status, prestige and access to positions of power. All will be hotly contested matters during a change period.

In addition, organizational theory has sensitized us to the power of lower order participants within organizations, those far removed from strategic decision-making positions. Experience shows that they may prevent change even while agreeing with it in general terms. Thus decentralization, widely acknowledged as a general principle making for greater flexibility and broadening participation in decision-making, has met with the hostility of groups at lower levels. They have frequently seen it as a threat to their centrally negotiated bargaining rights over pay and conditions of service and for increasing rather than decreasing the power exercised over them by their immediate managerial superiors. Such groups have fought hard to retain bureaucratic principles, even while accepting that they might make for inefficiency, on the grounds they provide both stability and safety.

Finally, the adoption of managerial rationality may founder in competition not only within departments but between them. The search for more effective systems of resource allocation for example, a key feature of the PESC system, has been based on the need to secure greater co-operation and agreement between departments on priorities. Yet, it remains true that budgeting and the distribution of resources is itself an area in which dispute and disagreement is rampant (Heclo and Wildavsky, 1974). Competition between departments for scarce resources has imposed an important constraint on the attempt to achieve unification between disparate departmental aims and objectives.

It would be wrong to end this chapter on a completely negative note. In spite of the fact that in some ways Fulton's proposals have been watered down, the committee did introduce important changes in departments consistent with the aims of a managerialist philosophy. In the next chapter we shall present a case study of change in an important department, the Post Office. The intention here is to illustrate the inevitable difficulties, contradictions and paradoxes involved in an attempt to replace bureaucratic/mechanistic principles of organization by their more organic alternatives, an attempt which involved the relocation of the functions of a government department in a public corporation.

Chapter 6

A CASE STUDY OF THE POST OFFICE

In 1969, following the proposal of the Fulton Committee that
accountable management might be 'most effectively introduced when
an activity is separately established outside any government
department' (see above, chapters 4 and 5), the Post Office was
formally hived off from the departmental system and reconstituted
as a public corporation – a form of 'semi-autonomous agency'
(Stanyer and Smith, 1976, p.55).   A little over ten years later we
can assess this experiment in 'de-bureaucratization'. It reveals
how significant a factor managerialism became. It demonstrates the
relevance of a mode of analysis which stresses the importance of
organizational conflict and politics. It discloses the contradictions in attempts to de-bureaucratize a central department,
even one with a commercial function for which a more flexible form
of organization was thought to be highly appropriate. Has this
change of status and location improved the efficiency of the former
department? What lessons does it hold for future hiving off
attempts? These issues form the central core of this chapter
(which is largely derived from Pitt, 1980).

A CHEQUERED HISTORY

As a department the Post Office had a long and venerable career
(Robinson, 1948). The origins of its postal monopoly may be traced
back to the days of the Tudor and Stuart monarchies. During the
nineteenth century it experienced a period of considerable expansion
of its executive activities. Its mail-carrying function was widened
to include not only letters but parcels. As a result of a High
Court ruling in 1869, it acquired the sole right to operate a
telegraph system throughout the country. In 1912, it became a
true 'ministry of communications' following its purchase of the
telephone business of private companies.
    However, this history of expansion was by no means unproblematical.
The department was subject to a constant backdrop of complaint
(particularly after 1912) both internally from its staff, and
externally from its customers. Examination of the many reports,
committees of inquiry and press campaigns which have littered its

development since that time reveals that its critics prophetically anticipated much later writing in organizational theory. In pointing to problems relating to departmental goals, structure, environment and technology, they unwittingly provided a contingency analysis of both posts and telecommunications.

After the First World War, frequent criticisms were voiced of the department's telecommunications policies. It was felt to be artificially restricting the development of the new medium. Its main goal, so it was asserted, should have been the muscular commercial exploitation of the telephone by stimulation of consumer demand and the simultaneous adoption of a large-scale capital investment programme. Instead, it was characterized as responding only reluctantly to spontaneous forces in its external environment. Following a growing press campaign aimed at exposing these policy weaknesses, a select committee was appointed in 1920 to examine the telephone service. Endorsing the widely held view that the department's goals were out of alignment with its environment, the committee also devoted considerable attention to the linked question of its internal structure. Its report suggested that there were major organizational weaknesses in the telephone function. The negative consequences of bureaucracy were very much in evidence.

State takeover of privately run telephone systems was a mixed blessing for the Post Office secretariat, the key decision-making group within the department. It had to decide whether to establish a dual system of administration under which postal and telecommunications officials would be kept entirely separate within their own 'command structures', or to integrate them both within a single unified system. In the event it chose the latter course on two basic grounds. First, the case was made that complete separation of personnel would lead to considerable duplication. The Post Office offers a nationwide system of posts and telecommunications. Advocates of a unified organizational structure pointed to the fact that complete service separation would force the department to construct telephone exchanges in distinct buildings, rather than use those already available in the provincial postal network on a 'joint user' basis. Linked to this was the objection that 'common service' costs would rise. Instead of posts and telecommunications sharing joint facilities for motor vehicle maintenance and garaging, for example, separate facilities would be required. The second factor was that of the presumed administrative inexperience of the technical staffs of private companies newly assimilated into the Post Office. These personnel should be placed under the overall direction of postal officials with detailed knowledge of departmental procedures and working practices. This 'safety first' strategy of organizational design was undoubtedly prompted by the Treasury. Exercising its influence as the department with final responsibility for machinery of government questions, it prevented the establishment of a separate telecommunications organization on the grounds that it would be both costly and disruptive of settled bureaucratic routines. As a result, the telecommunications echelons were placed firmly under postal control with a secretariat in London and surveyors in the provinces. Henceforth, specialist personnel - most notably engineers - would be subordinated to lay officials.

Internal dissatisfaction with this arrangement quickly grew.
Giving evidence before the select committee, members of the telecommunications grades pointed to serious organizational weaknesses.
They complained about the constant interference of postal officials
in decisions requiring technical expertise. In addition, they
suggested that the structure was too centralized. Having constantly
to refer matters upward through several organizational levels for
prior authorization, they were prevented from adopting a flexible
and speedy approach to telecommunications problems. In short, a
bureaucratic structure well enough adapted to the relatively
unchanging tasks of the postal service was unsuited to telecommunications, operating within a turbulent environment of increasing
consumer dissatisfaction and with a rapidly changing technology.

The failure of the department to respond to these criticisms led
to continuing negative comment. During the 1920s, a series of
pressure groups endeavoured to persuade it to adopt a more businesslike policy in relation to the telephone, arguing that there existed
a large pent-up environmental demand for the new medium which it
was failing to satisfy. Added force was given to this argument by
a prominent politician, Lord Wolmer. As an ex-Assistant Postmaster
General, he was well qualified to comment on the presumed failings
of the Post Office. He suggested that the department was hamstrung
in its efforts to increase the size of the telephone network by the
Treasury, which insisted on treating it as a revenue earner. It
was required to pay over the bulk of its receipts from postal and
telecommunications operations to the central Exchequer. Unlike a
business organization, it was denied capital from which to finance
investment in new telephone equipment. Without it, it could not
make financial provision for future long term growth. It was thus
subject to a process of goal displacement. Short-term financial
considerations drove out long-term planning.

Coupled with his views on unsatisfactory relationships with the
Treasury, Wolmer criticized the internal structure of the department.
He argued that a bureaucratic structure was unsuited for an
organization like the Post Office, selling its products (mail and
telephone services) to the public and requiring to respond
effectively to changing customer demand. He believed that improvements in the overall performance of the department would follow
from a radical reconstitution of its status. Rehearsing an argument
which was destined to gain prominence in later years, he suggested
that the Post Office should be removed from the departmental system
altogether and redesignated as a semi-autonomous agency. This
would relieve it from detailed ministerial, parliamentary and
Treasury control. Provided with a source of independent finance
it could engage in a stable, long-term programme of capital
investment. It would be free from short-term political and
financial pressures. In addition, it would be able to introduce
a more flexible form of internal organization constructed on the
principle that decision-making should be delegated to the lowest
possible levels. A more organic form of organization could thus be
substituted for a rigidly mechanistic one.

Criticism of the Post Office reached a crescendo at the beginning
of the 1930s. In response to this, the Postmaster General (the
minister with responsibility for the department) advised the Prime

Minister that a further committee of inquiry must be appointed. It
was conceded that change in the structure of the Post Office was
inevitable particularly in relation to its telecommunications
service. Accordingly, the Bridgeman Committee was set up. It was
prevented by its terms of reference from considering the possibility
of hiving off the department and relocating it as a semi-autonomous
agency. Nevertheless, it carried out extensive investigations of the
relationships existing between the department, Treasury and parliament
At the same time, it subjected its internal structure to detailed
critical review. The recommendations of the committee were destined
to have a considerable influence over the working of the department
for many years to come.

Its main object was to imbue the Post Office with a considerable
degree of financial independence - an essential element of any
business organization - while providing it with a high level of
internal organizational flexibility. It concurred with Wolmer's
view that the Treasury was effectively depriving the department of
much-needed revenue from which it might finance future capital
development (thus inhibiting expansion of the telephone network in
response to environmental demand). In this connection, too, the
committee accepted the fact that Treasury financial controls were
also a main contributor to the adoption within the Post Office of
a rigid bureaucratic structure. Here, the main problem was that the
Treasury insisted that its prior authorization was needed for
decisions involving expenditure, however small. This was particularly
troublesome in telecommunications, a highly capital-intensive
function. Not only were telecommunications officials required to
consult with higher level postal officials before embarking on work
involving capital outlays. The postal officials also had to seek
further endorsement by referring the matter outside the department
to the Treasury. Such a system reinforced negative bureaucratic
forces. It encouraged mistake avoidance rather than risk-taking
strategies and was both cumbersome and slow.

To combat such pathological tendencies, the committee proposed
a loosening up of the relationship between the two departments.
This would be achieved by the establishment of a Post Office Fund.
After making an agreed annual contribution to the Exchequer, the
department would be allowed to use its receipts for the 'benefit
of the public, the improvement of the services and the development
of its business'. Operating under the severe constraint that it
could not recommend hiving off as a solution to Post Office problems,
the committee none the less argued for fairly radical internal
organizational reform within the department.

In the committee's recommendations for organizational reform
may be seen a contingency logic. Accepting the main thrust of
Wolmer's argument that a more flexible form of organizational
structure should be adopted in the department as a whole, it
insisted that this was particularly necessary in telecommunications.
While a modified form of bureaucratic structure might be retained
in the postal organization (labour-intensive and highly routine)
the telecommunications function (capital intensive and utilizing a
technology subject to constant change and improvement and employing
large numbers of professional personnel) would require a much more
organic framework. Within an omnibus department embracing both

services, the committee pressed for maximum differentiation between them (see Lawrence and Lorsch, 1967). Each should be encouraged to adopt that form of organization best suited to its individual requirements.

Bridgeman well recognized, as had critics before it, that a major structural problem resided in the control of professional functionaries by lay personnel. To combat this tendency, it proposed major changes within the organization. In the first place, it concluded that the top level decision-making body - the secretariat - should be reconstituted. It was dominated by postal officials. Its most serious weakness was the exclusion of the engineer-in-chief (the key professional officer in telecommunications) from its membership. This meant that 'engineering experience (was) insufficiently brought into the consideration and formulation of general policy'. Second, changes were needed in the localities. Just as the secretariat perpetuated a regime of lay dominance over telephone personnel at the top of the organization, so too did the surveyors, the key cadre of provincial officials, at lower levels. They were unfitted by experience to understand the unique techno- logical and environmental problems in telecommunications. Their very presence militated against the adoption of an organizational system best designed to cope with them.

The changes which followed in the wake of the Bridgeman Report were strikingly modern. They were well in advance of much later contingency thinking on government organizations exemplified, for example, in the deliberations of the Fulton Committee. They constituted the first real attempt to imbue the Post Office with an organic/adaptive organizational format. The establishment of an independent Post Office Fund (again, in advance of the later trading funds set up in certain departmental agencies) lessened the degree of detailed Treasury control and its involvement in the minutiae of departmental decision-making. In important areas of policy involving financial matters, such as the construction of new telephone exchanges, departmental officials were given greater powers to operate without seeking prior approval. It was hoped that such a modification would encourage the introduction of general schemes of decentralization of authority within the Post Office. This could, in turn, encourage greater flexibility.

These changes were accompanied by important internal structural reforms. The headquarters organization was completely reconstituted. The secretariat was replaced by a board upon which sat representatives of the telecommunications organization. In the provinces, the office of surveyor was abolished and replaced with that of regional director. Given combined responsibility for the administration of postal and telecommunications services, this official was assisted by a board similar in composition to that at headquarters' level. Telecommunications personnel were represented on it. All this challenged a fundamental principle of bureaucratic organization in government departments, namely that 'professionals' should be subordinated to 'lay' personnel. Whereas, for example, the surveyors had previously been drawn exclusively from postal ranks, the new office of regional director would be accessible equally to telecommunications and postal personnel. By this means, it was hoped to deal with a problem of hierarchical inflexibility very much in operation in the pre-existing format.

Important new measures of organizational control were introduced, reminiscent of Fulton's accountable management, to encourage de-centralization. Headquarters' powers were restricted to those concerned with the maintenance of national standards (particularly important to ensure equity in provision and performance over the country as a whole). All other matters were dealt with independently by regional directors and below them area managers (telecommunications and head postmasters. To encourage maximum efficiency in such a decentralized system, bureaucratic methods of control were relinquished in favour of a system of financial and performance control, including a series of regional control accounts which would provide provincial officials 'with the necessary data to measure their own performance, compare it with that of colleagues in other areas, and be judged by it' (Pitt, 1980, p.81).

WAR AND ITS AFTERMATH

In spite of such a promising and modernistic approach to the problems of the department, the Second World War dealt a blow to hopes of a more flexible and responsive organizational format. While the regional reorganization was hurriedly brought into existence, the Treasury was adamant that the Post Office Fund must be relinquished. Determined that the Post Office must be treated like any other revenue-earning department for the duration, it suspended its operation. Thus, at a stroke, the financial independence of the department was attacked.

By the beginning of the 1950s, familiar complaints were re-emerging, both within the Post Office and outside it. It was suggested that the department could not plan effectively the future development of its services (long-term goals were prejudiced by short-term problems); it was even further out of alignment with environmental demands for better and more efficient service, and its internal structure was unsuited to its major tasks. These criticisms were aimed with particular force at the telecommunications organization.

As many historians have noted, war often forces the pace of social change in a country. This was evidently true in Britain. The population began to demand improvements in education, health and social services. For its part, the Post Office began to experience even stronger environmental pressures for greater and greater numbers of telephones. Yet it was precisely at this time that the department was least capable of responding to them. Its telephone development programme was subject to important constraints. The most immediate of these was the war itself. While encouraging the formation of a strong 'telephone habit' amongst the British public, it led to deterioration in equipment and line plant. Many tele-communications engineers were called up for military service and this meant that the exchanges and distribution network of the department received inadequate maintenance. Much equipment, destroyed by enemy action, had to be replaced. Thus the Post Office experienced a classic problem. Faced with growing demand, it was unable to match it with adequate supply.

The second and linked problem was that of government and Treasury

policy.   The accession to power of a Labour government in 1945 marked
the beginning of a period of considerable organizational innovation
at the central government level.   The government embarked upon a
nationalization programme, taking into state control the coal, gas,
iron and steel and railway industries.   Putting into practice the
ideas of one of its ministers, Herbert Morrison, it concluded that
orthodox departments were ill-suited for the administration of the
newly acquired functions.   Close ministerial supervision and control
were inimical to the development of services with clear commercial
characteristics.   Instead, an organizational solution had to be
devised which, while giving governments final authority, would allow
managements a high degree of operational and financial freedom.
The solution adopted was a semi-autonomous form of organization.
Ministers would be held at 'arm's length' on day-to-day matters,
intervening in internal affairs only so far as was necessary to
give general directions to managers on questions involving the
national interest.   The Treasury would be similarly constrained
from detailed and continuous intervention in the financial affairs
of the new corporations.

Members of the telecommunications organization looked on such an
arrangement with envy.   Compared with the Post Office, the
nationalized industries were guaranteed a high degree of freedom
from political and financial interference, both necessary conditions
for successful experimentation with organic systems of organization.
Critics within the department were quick to conclude that the Post
Office should be accorded similar semi-autonomous status.   Yet the
government declined to respond to this challenge.   The establishment
of public corporations was part of a party programme stressing the
necessity for taking over functions previously performed by private
sector organizations.   The question of hiving off the whole or parts
of departments such as the Post Office and relocating them in more
independent structures was not part of Labour's programme.   Such a
strategy would emerge only later.   Of equal significance was the
fact that communication services (and, in particular, telecommunications) were increasingly seen as an important component of the
defence system of the country.   It was widely accepted in government
circles that defence interests would be best served by locating
responsibility for them firmly within central departments under
the watchful eyes of ministers and Cabinet.

Finally, under the pressure of a developing adverse economic
climate, the Treasury refused to accord the department even the
measured degree of financial independence envisaged by Bridgeman
in the pre-War period.   An examination of the Post Office by the
Select Committee on Estimates provided encouragement to this view.
This reached the conclusion that, although the department would
undoubtedly benefit from the possession of an independent reserve
fund, such an arrangement was impossible in the strained economic
circumstances of the time.   To cope with a series of short-term
economic crises, the Chancellor of the Exchequer was forced to
adopt a policy of rigid capital allocation in the public sector.
He deemed it essential to divert resources to the export industry
to improve the country's balance of payments position.   This made
it necessary to reduce the level of investment in the domestic
telecommunications development programme.   At a time when internal

and external critics were once again pressing for greater freedom and flexibility within the department, it became the target of greater ministerial and Treasury intervention.

Criticisms of the department grew rather than diminished as the decade progressed. As in previous years, these focused primarily on the telecommunications organization. To the voices of consumer groups complaining about the indifferent quality of telephone service (due both to inadequate finance and the resulting failure to apply new technical innovations) were added those of groups within the department critical of a mismatch which they perceived between organizational structure and a changing technology. One of the most important of these was the Post Office Engineering Union representing the bulk of the engineering workforce. Contrary to the view of the Lumley Committee, which suggested in 1950 that the structure of the department was broadly in keeping with the effective management of its various services, the POEU complained that the organization of the telecommunications function was still subject to inappropriate postal (lay) direction. Telephone managers, for example, did not have full control of their operating force. Telephone operators were, in fact, subject on disciplinary matters to the local head postmaster. More significantly, the traditional fault of bureaucratic structures, over-centralization, was still very much a force to be reckoned with. In spite of the professed intention of the Bridgeman reforms to push decision-making authority down to the lowest levels in the department in the interest of encouraging flexibility, headquarters was frequently unwilling to concede this principle. Paradoxically, bureaucratic practices had become even further entrenched.

Force was added to such criticisms by a revolutionary series of technological developments. The most important of these was subscriber trunk dialling (STD). In 1957, the government announced that it would introduce a programme of automation of the 'most sweeping and radical kind'. This would cut out the need for telephone operators to connect subscribers when making calls. A machine-operated telephone network would eventually supersede a manually operated one. Speed in connection and less incorrectly routed calls were the hoped for results. There was wide acceptance within the department that the introduction of this scheme would have important organizational implications. In 1959 a joint study group of Post Office management and trade union representatives visited the United States to examine the American Bell Telephone Company. Since the Second World War, this privately owned company supplying telephone services had experienced a huge growth in its domestic market. Unlike the Post Office, it had managed to keep up with increasing environmental demand. Success in supplying an ever-increasing number of telephones was matched by its ability to improve the technical efficiency of its operations. Ninety-two per cent of its telephones were connected to automatic exchanges.

The major finding of the study group was the revelation that automation had increased the necessity within the company for the adoption of flexible organizational practices. The group therefore concluded that the American company was well adapted for dealing with rapid technological changes of the kind currently facing the Post Office. In essence, Bell had abandoned rigid bureaucratic procedures in favour of the assumption of more organic alternatives. Rigid demarcation between lay and professional workers had been actively prevented. Instead individuals with a technical background were encouraged to compete for top management posts, ensuring that engineering considerations were fully taken into account at the summit of the organization. It thus had successfully prevented the establishment of rigid barriers between different occupational groups, a key negative feature of bureaucratic organizations. The adoption of practices bearing close affinity to those of accountable management further encouraged organizational flexibility. Rewards were strictly related to performance.

With this example firmly in mind, the study group concluded that new forms of organizational control and better measures of individual and group performance should be established in the British system. The adoption of a more organic organizational structure within telecommunications would both increase its ability to respond to consumer demand (still increasing) while simultaneously allowing its technological modernization. Reflecting on organizational weaknesses at the end of the decade, the POEU concluded that the rapid growth of technological innovations such as STD had subjected the Post Office to structural strain. Giving evidence before yet another study group (the Wolverson Committee) which was inquiring into organizational malfunctioning, the union concluded that reforms were necessary. The most important of these was that telecommunications - an overtly technological system - should be prised loose from the grip of lay personnel. Thus relieved, the function should be further adapted by the removal of artificial hierarchical divisions within it which were preventing its effective internal integration (see Lawrence and Lorsch, 1967). The union instanced what it felt to be an unnecessary division of responsibility between engineers and traffic officers which meant that the organization displayed problems of 'bureaucratic rigidity [and] overlapping and inadequate functional co-operation' (Pitt, 1980, p.117).

As with the 1930s, the 1950s was a decade of disillusion with the methods and organizational practices of the department. This was further encouraged by the failure of such reform schemes as were introduced. Stung into action by continuing criticisms of the Post Office, the government produced a highly influential White Paper on its finances in 1955. This appeared to mark a return to the principles of Bridgemanism. Recognizing that the long-term aims of the department were consistently prejudiced by lack of adequate finance, the White Paper established the rule that in the future the Post Office would be expected to contribute a relatively modest annual sum to the Treasury (£5m). Revenue accruing above that amount would be carried forward to form a reserve fund. This expedient would, it was hoped, allow the department a greater degree of freedom from Treasury intervention. While it would continue to have an obligation to consult the Treasury on matters raising important or novel issues, the Treasury, for its part, would desist from commenting on the finer points of day-to-day administration.

An important objective of the White Paper lay in its commitment to the philosophy of planning. The Post Office should be allowed to plan the future growth of its business over a series of three-year periods. This was particularly important for a capital-intensive function like telecommunications in which decisions about investment had major long-term implications. However, the good intentions of the White Paper were quickly compromised. The optimistic plans of the department to extend its investment programme in accordance with the expressed intention of the White Paper were nullified by events. Continuing balance of payments problems forced the Cabinet to cut back the rate of investment in the public sector generally. The implications of this policy were felt particularly severely in the Post Office. Levels of investment in new plant and equipment declined steadily until the beginning of the 1960s.

Disappointments with attempts to improve the financial standing of the Post Office were linked to others arising out of reviews of its internal structure. The observation contained in the Wolverson Report that the telecommunications organization of the 1930s 'was well adapted to the fully automatic system' of the 1950s conveyed an impression of departmental unwillingness to support much needed organizational reform. The failure of the report to recommend changes in the hierarchical structure of telecommunications was seen by the POEU as reactionary.

Unsurprisingly, these failures had the effect of radicalizing reform demands. Until mid-decade, the POEU, for example, had contented itself with proposing changes within the context of a largely undisturbed departmental framework. The 1955 White Paper had appeared to promise much greater organizational flexibility and freedom. It therefore seemed redundant to press for a more radical policy of separating the Post Office entirely from the departmental system and reconstituting it as a semi-independent agency. Recoiling from the hammer-blow of continuing disappoint-ments, the union dedicated itself wholeheartedly to a more fundamental solution to the problems of the department along these lines. Determined to bring the policy of the government into line with this revised thinking (an interesting example of members of a department seeking to influence an important part of their environment) it won support from an unexpected source.

In 1959 a new Conservative government was elected. Included among its members was Ernest Marples, a minister with wide experience of private sector management. He was appointed to the office of Postmaster General. It was evident that he had strongly held views on the working of the department. He was instrumental in persuading the Conservative Party that it should include in its election manifesto a proposal for freeing the Post Office from over-zealous Treasury supervision. Marples' influence was also revealed in the commitment of the party to consider the department as a commercial organization. As a key member of the strategic coalition in the Post Office he endorsed the view of the union that bureaucratic structures should be replaced, so far as was possible, by organic counterparts. Statements which he made after leaving office made clear his view that wholesale reform would follow on from a commitment to fundamental constitutional change. He was an early and ardent supporter of hiving off.

THE 1960s - MANAGERIALISM REVISITED

We argued in the previous chapter that the 1960s was a decade during
which managerialism became widely accepted. Events were to show
that the Post Office was not immune from its influence. Indeed,
the change in status of the Post Office in 1969 which removed it
from the departmental system was premised on the feeling that hiving
off would encourage the adoption of the best in private sector
management practices.

In 1961 yet another White Paper was published. Showing every
sign of Marples' authorship, it declared in favour of the adoption
of a more businesslike framework for the running of departmental
services. The Post Office, it announced, should be encouraged
to 'innovate and develop as a business, seeking to meet and
anticipate its customers' demands'. Consistent with the earlier
document in 1955, it announced the intention of the government to
revive the idea of a Post Office Trading Fund. Once again, it was
stated that freedom from detailed Treasury control was a prime
objective. It hoped that a measure of independence would encourage
the adoption of up to date management methods and a general
improvement in internal working practices. Unlike the 1955 White
Paper, the proposals contained in this later document were backed
up by legislative enactment. Following its appearance, a Post
Office Act was published. While rejecting the idea of hiving off
as too radical a policy, the Act recognized the special difficulties
facing the department. It sought to encourage the abandonment of
largely negative 'mistake avoidance' decision-making strategies
and attendant bureaucratic weaknesses - particularly over-centralization. Instead, it hoped to foster commitment to a more entrepreneurial, 'success-seeking' managerial philosophy and organic
organizational practices.

Once again, disappointment quickly followed. Rejecting hiving
off, the Act had, in fact, conferred hybrid status on the Post
Office. It would remain a department - one, however, with many of
the features of a semi-independent agency. It was true that this
provided it with a greater degree of freedom from detailed Treasury
oversight and financial control, putting it roughly on a par with
the nationalized industries. It was also true that important
changes in internal structure followed on from the Act; new forms
of organizational control had been developed enabling the better
definition of objectives and the measurement of performance. Yet,
its continued constitutional status as a department of state
contained the distinct possibility that ministers would seek to
intervene directly in its day-to-day affairs, inhibiting management
from taking decisions on a purely commercial basis. Similarly,
detailed parliamentary oversight would incline management to be
over-cautious in the development of departmental policy.

The vulnerability of the department to continued outside
interference was readily apparent.   In 1962, a worsening
economic climate induced the government, once again, to adopt
restrictionist financial policies in the public sector. The Post
Office was faced with successive expenditure cuts in its capital
investment programme. Financial independence was a myth. To make
matters worse, the reforming Postmaster General Ernest Marples was

replaced by Reginald Bevins who appeared not to harbour the same
vision of a thrusting dynamic organization. His view that the Post
Office should not actively stimulate further demand for the telephone,
for example, was fully in keeping with the financial orthodoxy of
the time. The internal pressures for more independence and
flexibility to face changing technological and environmental
circumstances foundered against Bevins's determination that consumer
demands for the telephone should be suppressed. He thus rejected
arguments in favour of the adoption of a more organic form of
organization to meet a changing environment. Bevins's policy reveals
the power of strategic decision-makers to choose how environmental
needs are to be defined and the type of organizational response to
be made.

Two factors salvaged the hopes of reformers for schemes of
organizational change. The first was the development amongst
governments of all political persuasions of a belief in the philosophy
of planning (we have already seen that this was central to a
managerialist ideology). The second was the election of a Labour
administration in 1964 which quickly announced its commitment to a
programme of organizational renewal in the public sector.

The Conservative government, of which Bevins was a member,
embarked in 1962 on a policy of indicative planning. Selwyn Lloyd,
the Chancellor of the Exchequer, set up the National Economic
Development Council (NEDC) with the object of establishing a
concordat between government, employers and unions to discuss
obstacles to economic growth and the related question of achieving
a planned expansion in economic activities. The NEDC, viewing the
Post Office as having a major part to play in this, pointed to
important organizational weaknesses within it. It supported the
widely held view that short sighted government policy was preventing
the development of a stable system of long-term planning. Similarly,
it insisted that the department was not keeping pace with increasing
environmental demand. Finally, outmoded organizational practices
were in evidence.

The appearance in 1963 of a further White Paper, this time on the
telephone service, marked a change of heart on the part of the
government. Announcing a 'massive increase in capital investment
within the context of a five year plan', it declared an intention
to cut the size of the waiting list for telephone installations.
Such an aim was in keeping with the wishes of departmental critics
for a much more aggressive policy of service expansion.

The return to power of a Labour government in 1964 heralded a
further improvement in departmental fortunes. The Labour Party
election manifesto placed great emphasis on the need to bring about
a scientific and technological revolution in Britain and to
revitalize the country's flagging industrial performance record.
The Post Office seemed poised to benefit from this philosophy.
Rapid technological development in communications would be of
central importance to such a revolution, a point which had not
escaped the attention of commentators for many years.

The department was fortunate, at this time in its history, in
the appointment to the office of Postmaster General of Anthony
Wedgewood Benn. It acquired in him an able minister and one
committed, moreover, to schemes of organizational change and

development. Realizing this, the telecommunications unions were
quick to impress on him their view that further changes in structure
and organization were necessary. The POEU, for example, insisted
that, in spite of the formal changes which had occurred with the
passage of the 1961 Act, the department displayed characteristically
negative bureaucratic features. The union argued that direct
ministerial answerability to parliament for the detailed affairs of
the department inhibited management and led to caution and delay in
decision-making. The Treasury, too, was castigated. Still denying
the Post Office adequate finance, it exercised close control over
its internal affairs. Typically, the result was over-centralization.

Responding to such views, Wedgewood Benn announced the establishment of an inquiry into the internal structure of the department
by a firm of industrial consultants (McKinsey's). At the same time
he held out the hope of more generous allocations of finance by the
government for the development of Post Office services, particularly
telecommunications. Further encouragement came with the publication
in 1965 of an ambitious National Plan drawn up by the government.
Projecting a 25 per cent increase in economic activity by 1970, the
document predicted a dramatic increase in the level of Post Office
activities. Its telecommunications business would expand by 11 per
cent per annum to the end of the decade. Its investment programme
would double in size to enable it to keep pace with a continuing
growth in environmental demand for the telephone.

In the same year, the NEDC established a committee ('little
Neddy') to discuss the means by which the department could achieve
more effective goal attainment. It concluded that a greater
commitment to long-term planning was necessary. Linked to this
was its recommendation that the internal organization should be
revamped. In particular, it observed that the telecommunications
organization was experiencing considerable strain as it strove
to keep up with environmental pressures. Once again, contingency
logic was very much in evidence. Telecommunications services
should be organized along much more flexible lines. This was
impossible in a departmental structure which encouraged bureaucratic
rigidity. Posts and telecommunications should be much more clearly
differentiated. Each had unique operating characteristics. Within
telecommunications, a rationalization of hierarchical divisions
should take place. Tasks should be grouped on a functional basis.
Clear cut criteria of performance should be established. A more
organic organizational structure was essential. Support for such
a view came in the report of the McKinsey inquiry. It, too,
concluded that the structure of the department should be made more
organic. A traditional bureaucratic structure was inappropriate
to the development of modern communications systems. Placing
their faith in a hiving off strategy, the consultants took the
further step of advocating not the establishment of one semi-
autonomous agency but two; one for posts, the other for telecommunications. The POEU and other telecommunications unions were quick to
endorse this view, seeing in it the chance to insulate themselves
completely from postal interference.

The decision to establish some form of hived-off agency was
taken in 1965. Meanwhile the department was subjected to further
scrutiny. In 1966, the Select Committee on the Nationalized

Industries carried out a detailed investigation of the department. While its deliberations appear to have had little influence on the eventual process of hiving off, they provide important evidence of the influence of academic organizational theory on the thinking of departmental members. For example, in giving evidence before the committee, the POEU quoted the work of Joan Woodward in support of its plea that more organic working practices were required for the handling of complex technological tasks such as those involved in telecommunications. In fact, critics of the Post Office, both within and outside it, supported the view that the organization remained inflexible. Treasury and parliamentary supervision had discouraged initiative and enterprise. Over-centralization, inappropriate differentiation between services, and inadequate integration between hierarchies within the telecommunications organization were cited in time-honoured fashion as faults of a civil service bureaucratic structure. Such a structure was completely at variance with the needs of an organization facing a turbulent environment and dealing with a rapidly changing technology.

Rejecting the idea of setting up two agencies as 'too draconian', the committee nevertheless responded positively to such criticism. It pressed for the establishment of an agency along lines similar to those for the nationalized industries. Managers would be relieved from detailed parliamentary, Treasury and ministerial control. Given a degree of financial independence, they would be able to develop the services of the department along strictly business lines. The committee argued that, within such an omnibus agency, the principle should be adopted of separating out the two services. Coupled with a thoroughgoing system of devolved authority, such separation would allow each service to be run strictly in accordance with its individual needs.

THE ESTABLISHMENT OF THE POST OFFICE CORPORATION

The process of legislative reform which began in 1961 conferring hybrid status on the department was completed in 1969. In that year, a further Act was passed removing the Post Office from the departmental system and re-designating it as a public corporation (semi-autonomous agency). Earlier, in 1967, the government made clear the objectives of this reform. It would complete a process of organizational change with origins as far back as the Bridgeman Report. A standard departmental form was 'unsuited to the running of the postal and telecommunications services'. The basic aim of this latest reform was the construction of a flexible, dynamic organization capable of responding well to environmental and technological pressures. Public corporation status would confer on the Post Office a degree of managerial freedom never before experienced. Like a business, it would be expected to pay its way and build up a financial reserve from which to fund future capital investment. Having been granted considerable independence from Treasury control in 1961 in accordance with this aim, the department would now be freed from close parliamentary and ministerial supervision. In line with Fultonian philosophy, the government suggested that hiving off would enable the adoption of accountable

management. Clear responsibilities would be assigned to individuals
within the new corporation for the achievement of clearly defined
objectives. Management by objectives would promote better motivation.
A 'sharpened sense of purpose and urgency' would be encouraged. The
last would be enhanced by the employment of a more organic form of
structure.

With these ends in view, the Act vested detailed overall responsibility for both posts and telecommunications in the hands of a
chairman and board at the apex of the organization, justifying this
approach on the principle that both services should be developed
together as part of an integrated communications policy. Nevertheless,
it suggested that, within the combined organization, maximum
differentiation between posts and telecommunications should occur in
the interest of separate development. To achieve this objective,
each service should be placed under the control of a managing
director reporting to the central board. Assisted by their own -
subordinate - boards, they would be given wide responsibilities
and all the support services needed to develop their functions.
While the corporation would be ultimately responsible to the
government through a sponsoring minister (originally the minister
for Posts and Telecommunications, later the Secretary of State
for Industry) he would be held at 'arm's length'. He would not be
expected to concern himself with the fine details of corporation
policy, but would only intervene on matters concerning the national
interest.

Change in the internal structure of the organization occurred
as a result of the alteration in departmental status. Indeed, even
in advance of the Act, important reforms were well under way. In
1968, when it was clear that the government was serious in its
intention to hive off the department, important alterations occurred
at top levels. These were designed to clarify hierarchical
responsibilities and achieve the maximum possible separation of the
two major functions. A management services unit was introduced at
headquarters level (in accordance with a recommendation of the
Fulton committee) to ensure that the organization was adopting up
to date management techniques. Linked to this was an important
rationalization of top level management salary structures as part
of the effort to introduce a practical and effective system of
management by objectives. The development of a Management Data
System (MDS) was designed to encourage accountable management. It
led to the establishment of cost and quality centres within each
major service.

Finally, important changes took place in the provincial organization. The most significant of these was a splitting up of the old
composite Bridgeman regions into separate units for posts and
telecommunications under their own regional directors in the
interest of encouraging greater differentiation between them.
Accompanying this, important reforms in the regional hierarchies
took place designed to achieve better integration between specialisms
such as traffic and engineering within each business.

When the Act finally became law, many of these processes were
accelerated. In 1970, for example, an important experiment in
regional organization was conducted. Two regions (one for posts,
the other for telecommunications) were established in an effort to

decentralize the organization further. Their success prompted the board of the corporation to embark on a radical policy of devolution of authority. Henceforth, a federal provincial structure would be introduced. Returning to the spirit of 'Bridgemanism', this would give regional directors considerably more authority and responsibility for the conduct of Post Office business in the provincial postal and telecommunications networks. Headquarters only had reserve powers to deal with exceptional circumstances. Such a system, it was felt, would encourage a significant relaxation of headquarters control and remove a major impediment to organizational flexibility - over centralization.

Other reforms of major significance accompanied this. To improve the goal-setting and attainment capabilities of the organization, a system of corporate planning was introduced. Its major aim was better strategic performance. It laid down a series of long-term objectives and monitored the activity of personnel in their achievement. To this end, a long-range studies division was set up in telecommunications headquarters. It was concerned with the drafting of long-term business objectives through a series of ten-year plans and was adamant that the corporation must be responsive to environmental, economic and technological change. To ensure that all parts of the corporation were working well together in the implementation of the plans, a business planning committee was established.

The development of such a planning machinery, designed to improve goal achievement in the organization, was matched by further organizational changes to bring the internal structure of the corporation into line with technology and environment. Progress with new motivational devices such as accountable management and management by objectives continued. The introduction of such schemes was undoubtedly aided by the fact that, with the arrival of corporation status, the Post Office was given much greater freedom in personnel matters than previously. It took over important personnel functions previously exercised on its behalf by the Civil Service Department. As Fulton had suggested, greater autonomy in establishments matters was a prerequisite for the successful implementation of schemes of accountable management.

Finally, the attempt continued to render the structure of the organization in both posts and telecommunications more flexible. Efforts were made to break up still further rigid hierarchical compartmentalism. Just as important changes took place in civil service grading structures in the wake of the Fulton Report, so it was hoped that the move to corporation status would open up positions throughout the Post Office to individuals regardless of their particular backgrounds. This was a move obviously designed to improve the promotion prospects of specialist personnel and encourage their advancement to top level posts previously the monopoly preserve of generalist administrators.

ORGANIZATIONAL ANALYSIS AND HIVING OFF

Hiving off, then, was a deliberate attempt to improve the goal-attainment capability of the Post Office and bring its structure

more closely into line with important contingencies, particularly
environment and technology. What light does contemporary organizational analysis throw on this constitutional transformation?

The first point that might be made is that contingency analysis –
an important paradigm in much recent academic writing on organizations –
is particularly relevant to an understanding of developments in the
department culminating in the 1969 change in its constitution. Study
of Post Office history, particularly since the time of the telephone
takeover in 1912, shows quite clearly that both internal and external
critics of the department have expended considerable energy arguing
that its structure has been frequently out of phase with both
environmental and technological change. The relevance of a
contingency theory approach in organizational analysis may be gauged
from the fact that groups concerned with the effectiveness of the
Post Office as a provider of communications services talked the
language of contingency theory long in advance of its development
as a dominant perspective in organizational analysis. Such a view
was particularly evident in relation to the telecommunications
function. It has long been assumed that while greater organizational
flexibility might improve the administration of a routine function
such as posts, it is absolutely essential to telecommunications.
Since 1920 the argument has tirelessly been deployed that this has
been a retarded service. In comparison with foreign experience,
the spread and development of the telecommunications medium has been
slow and protracted. There have been two aspects to this. First,
so it has been claimed, the Post Office has been dilatory in
providing telephones in quantities sufficient to satisfy a
consistently growing, and at times explosive, environmental demand.
Second, while telecommunications engineers within the Post Office
have equalled and occasionally surpassed the achievements of their
counterparts abroad in producing technical innovations, the Post
Office has again been backward in applying them, and so improving
the service. Just as the quantity of service available to the
subscriber has been retarded, so too has improvement in its quality.

The tenor of such criticisms may be revealed by examination of
the many reports and committees of inquiry to which the Post Office
has been subjected since the state takeover of the telephone business
of private companies. It was evident in the select committee report
in 1921 which castigated the department for applying bureaucratic
logic to essentially business problems. Departmental ethos and
structure were both unsuited to the rapid advancement of telecommunications. Wolmer's insistence that 'government/commercial'
functions required different organizational structures to
'government/administrative' functions (anticipating by nearly five
decades Keeling's (1972) argument that 'management' structures
should supersede 'administrative' structures where flexibility was
a major requirement) revealed an identical concern. Similarly,
Bridgeman's recommendations were founded on the contingency argument
that alternatives to a bureaucratic structure must be canvassed.
This theme re-emerged in the post-war years. Continuing setbacks
to the hopes of critics in those years led, as we have noted, to
their increased radicalism. Thwarted in their ambition of achieving
a loosening up of structure within a departmental context, they
pressed the contingency argument to its logical conclusion, that of

hiving off the Post Office and relocating it within a semi-autonomous
agency. Some went even further and insisted that two such agencies
should be established to achieve maximum service separation. It was
during this period, too, that the writings of academic organizational
theorists employing contingency analysis became of direct relevance
to the Post Office. Its most articulate critics, notably the POEU,
were well aware of the work of Woodward, Burns and Stalker and others,
and were determined to use it as supporting evidence for their view
that discrete organizational structures should be set up for posts
and telecommunications outside the confines of a traditionaal
departmental format.

But, if the history of the department reveals the strength and
relevance of contingency analysis in understanding the problems of
large organizations in the public sector, it also suggests that it
is insufficient on its own for an adequate understanding of their
complexity. While it is true that organizations are in part the
product of technological and environmental forces, or at the very
least are affected by them, they are also social and political
systems. As Strauss and others (1973) have claimed, they are 'systems
of negotiated order' in which debate, conflict and disagreement take
place. We suggested in chapter 4 that an important corrective to
contingency analysis has been developed by Child (1972). He has
noted that structure is not simply determined by a set of environmental and technological 'givens'. On the contrary, it is
constructed and reconstructed to an important degree as a result
of choices exercised by the strategic coalition within the organization. Leaders may encourage structural change to bring the organization into line with technological and environmental developments.
Or, just as likely, they may ignore them, damp them down, or
routinize them. In the interests of avoiding the unsettling effects
of technological and environmental change, they may resort to the
retention of bureaucratic structural forms. By extending Child's
analysis, it is possible to show that choice within an organization
about the structure to be adopted is not the sole prerogative of
the top level strategic coalition. Groups throughout the organization command important power resources which they will wield to
pursue their own objectives. While some of these groups may welcome
structural change, seeing in it important organizational and group
advantages, others may take a diametrically opposed stance, viewing
it as threatening and disruptive. The result, as organizational
theorists are now only too well aware, will be twofold. First,
disputes and conflicts will emerge. As one group promotes change,
another will resist it. They will have competing aims and goals.
Second, as a consequence of this, progress from one form of structure
to another will be halting and piecemeal.

The most striking fact about movement within the Post Office to
a more flexible organic structure has been its lengthy and drawn out
character. In spite of the sophistication of arguments in the early
years of this century in favour of organizational change, they have
taken over fifty years to come to fruition. Indeed, it is doubtful
that the change process has been completed. Even now voices are
being raised both within and outside the corporation for yet further
reforms. This suggests that hiving off is not the final solution
to the problems of the Post Office.

From the earliest years, moves to de-bureaucratize the department met with opposition, from above and below. At top decision-making levels within the Post Office doubts about the wisdom of according greater freedom and flexibility to the telecommunications cadres have long been in evidence. The Post Office secretariat frequently adopted a conservative posture on the question of organizational structure. The Treasury was also unwilling to acquiesce in the more radical step of establishing a separate organizational identity for the service. Successive Postmasters General have similarly responded negatively to pressures for change.

The main factors inhibiting the leadership from acquiescing in the development of more organic organizational forms have been economic and constitutional. Financial constraint and the require-ments of ministerial accountability both influenced the thinking of the strategic coalition. Leadership groups within the Post Office have chosen to interpret technological and environmental forces in a radically different way from that of their critics. While the latter pictured the environment of the department as turbulent the dominant coalition affected to see it as placid. For example, the strategic policy-makers denied that the 'telephone habit' had caught on in this country as it had elsewhere. For them the rapid extension of the telecommunications system and consequent reorganiza-tion would have to wait until changes had occurred in social custom.

The logic of arguing that since the environment was stable organic procedures were unnecessary, was a convenient device by means of which the strategic coalition (Treasury, Cabinet and Post Office management) could seek refuge in the sanctuary of existing bureaucratic procedures. It was thus able to contain demands for greater organizational flexibility. It was only with the arrival of the 1960s that the choice of leadership groups could be expanded to encompass the idea of more extensive departmental reform. Under the impact of planning and managerialist philosophies, schemes of organizational reform came into 'good currency', if belatedly.

But if de-bureaucratization depended to an important degree on the policies, choices and values of groups at the top of the organization, the history of the department suggests that the success of schemes of organizational change is similarly dependent on those of groups further down the hierarchy. Just as such schemes are vulnerable to macro economic and political forces, they may depend for their success or failure on the micro political system within the organization. Here recent organizational analysis is useful. Developments in this literature (for example, Crozier, 1964) have drawn attention to patterns of behavioural inconsistency on the part of 'lower order participants' which may produce a vicious circle. While agreeing that organizational change might lead to greater overall effectiveness, such groups frequently resist it on the grounds that it brings disadvantages to their members. The result may well be that greater efforts to make the organization more flexible produce equal forces making for bureaucratization. The organization cannot, as a result, easily escape its past.

The case of the Union of Postal Workers is a classic example of such a tendency. Representing the bulk of the labour force in the postal service, the UPW has responded to calls for greater

organizational flexibility with hesitancy and occasional hostility.
The reasons for this are not hard to find. Change has been seen
as threatening to its members. During the 1920s for example, the
union rightly feared that proposals to introduce an organic organization would lead to the loss of postal control over telecommunications.
In turn, this would result in the diminution of status of postal
personnel in comparison with their telecommunications counterparts.
Sharing the growing conviction that organizational improvements
were necessary in the Post Office, the union was nevertheless driven
to resist even moderate proposals for raising the status of
professional engineers. It fought hard, too, against suggestions
that the work of the department should be relocated in a semi-
autonomous agency. In this it allied itself to conservative opinion
in the secretariat, insisting that close parliamentary control over
the department's affairs should be retained to ensure that the Post
Office remained properly accountable to public opinion. Wolmer was
quick to point out that the UPW was like a drunkard, refusing to
let go of the bottle that was killing him. Preaching the virtues
of a more flexible and dynamic organization, it supported, in effect,
the very bureaucratic practices which made this aim impossible to
achieve.

During the 1930s a characteristic UPW stance developed which was
destined to re-emerge in later years. It reacted with hostility to
Bridgeman's suggestion that greater decentralization could be
encouraged in the organization through the medium of devolving more
powers from the centre to regional directors. The union could,
with justice, point to genuine dangers in such a policy. If
regional directors were allowed to vary standards within their
regions, this could result in a breach in the traditional principle
of equity. The department was expected to provide the same quality
of service to its customers throughout the United Kingdom. A less
noble objective was the protection of the union's centrally
negotiated bargaining rights. It declared itself opposed in principle
to any attempt to give regional management greater control over
issues related to conditions of service and rewards - both functional
requirements of any system of accountable management.

During the later change period in the 1960s, the union once
again rehearsed many of its earlier objections to organizational
change. While paying lip-service to the concept of an organic
organization, it once again pressed for the retention of mechanistic
structures. Its main fear at this time lay in the emerging proposals
to separate out the post and telecommunications functions completely
and relocate them in separate hived off agencies. As Bealey (1976)
has shown, the union was able to exert sufficient pressure on the
government to prevent the adoption of a scheme which many reformers
thought essential to better performance. It undoubtedly felt that
while an independent telecommunications organization would reap the
benefits of growth, thus attracting steadily increasing government
finance, its members would be left in a declining rump postal
organization. Likewise, the union has consistently turned its back
on schemes of work measurement and accountable management, again on
the grounds that they would interfere with its members' rights of
access to headquarters. Willing the ends of a more businesslike
organization, it has been seemingly unable to endorse the means
necessary for its attainment.

The telecommunications organization, too, has manifested such tendencies. The development of full automation in the telephone system in the late 1950s was welcomed by the telecommunications engineers. Once again, it promised a rise in status of professional groups. Its organizational consequences - the break-up of old hierarchical divisions and lowering of prestige for other groups - was successfully resisted for some time by traffic officers, as we have seen. They too had endorsed the general objective of a more flexible, dynamic organization.

The lessons of a politically informed account of organizations are that change within them may be an exceptionally difficult matter. Recent experience in the Post Office during the 1960s and 1970s highlights some of these difficulties. The literature on the management of change has pointed increasingly to the resistance that innovations generate. The process of implementing reorganization has to be carried through carefully. Conflict is an important element in this. A pluralistic view of organizations also emphasizes goal conflict in times of change. This is related to the uncertainty created by change for organizational members. One way of coping with uncertainty is to retreat to the predictability of bureaucratic procedures and rules. The dilemma in escaping from bureaucracy is that the process is accompanied by demands for the conservation of existing structures as well as by conflicts of interest.

In the Post Office there was apparent consensus that change was desirable. Managerialism appeared to be a programme which could dissolve conflict and unite interests behind the single goal of efficiency. We are now witnessing the re-emergence of goal conflict which has not been removed by formal organizational change. For example, it was hoped that hiving off would improve industrial relations which had deteriorated during the 1950s and early 1960s. Union expectations of an improved climate of industrial relations were encouraged by changing government attitudes towards the department. These gave rise to a general feeling of optimism about the Post Office, and the unions endorsed the managerialist programme.

Consensus, however, was soon threatened by changes in government policy, particularly in relation to pay and trade union law. In addition, although management claimed to be moving towards a more open and consultative decision making process, the unions denied this. They claimed that structural changes such as the adoption of management by objectives, were being introduced without prior consultation. Thus, the move towards a more flexible organization appeared to be implemented in a unilateral and authoritarian manner.

Though there had originally been broad agreement on the ideology of managerialism the unions soon realized that the realities of reorganization produced results which conflicted with their values, such as the principle of equitable service provision and their own interest in negotiating and bargaining procedures.

Conflict over these issues increased after hiving off. The unions claimed that 'primitive relationships' had been imported from private industry. The changed atmosphere expected from the reforms did not materialize. Management, for its part, viewed trade union attitudes as being unhelpful claiming that they obstructed change and blocked the delegation of authority to area

and local levels. Reforms regarded as essential for accountable
management, such as mixed hierarchies, encountered union opposition.
Relations between traffic officers and engineers, for example,
worsened. Each group actively tried to retain its own organizational
identity. Thus the principles to which all paid lip-service failed
at the implementation stage. A climate of distrust grew and pervaded
the atmosphere of the new corporation. The result was the organization
became caught in a vicious circle. The more unhelpful the unions
appeared to management, the more it relied on a unilateral process
of decision-making. The more it relied on this, the less co-operative
the unions became. These difficulties were exacerbated by worsening
relationships between the corporation and the government, including
the sacking of the Post Office Chairman over important policy
disagreements and a strike by postal workers against government pay
policy. A decade after these developments a commentator on the
postal function (Corby, 1979) has pointed to continuing problems with
industrial relations.

Problems such as these have led to the retention of a bureaucratic
structure which remains unsuited to task and technological potential.
A negative feature of this structure is over-centralization. A
general erosion of initiative has followed. At board level management
still appears to place heavy reliance on rules preventing 'the
exercise of common sense' (Carter Committee, 1977) and the development of self-critical attitudes, encouraging instead adherence to
established positions long after they have ceased to be defensible.
Management has also proved weak in moving the organization in new
directions.

Attempts to decentralize the organization have met with little
success. Management has admitted that the delegation of authority
beyond regional level has proved impossible because of union
intransigence. The unions for their part have argued that even
regional decentralization has been something of a failure. The
attempt to construct a new regional system along federal lines has
been compromised by management's determination to extend the reserve
powers of headquarters. Evidence given to the Carter Committee by
the CBI indicates in addition that the splitting of regional
functions has perpetuated unnecessary tiers in the structure, so
distorting communication and increasing bureaucratic rigidity.
The resulting diffusion of responsibility has caused administrative
muddle.

Centralized decision-making has proved inappropriate to the
development of a truly commercial operation. A measure of this
failure is the well documented deterioration in customer relationships (Carter Committee, 1977 and Corby, 1979). Final authority
is too far removed from the point at which the service is delivered.
The centralization of industrial relations, of dubious value before
hiving off, is now positively dysfunctional. There are indications,
too, that the growth in numbers of headquarters and regional
management personnel is producing a top-heavy organization.

The new status of the Post Office has not led to more effective
structural co-ordination. The management of important technological
projects has been prejudiced by an inappropriate division of labour
in telecommunications. Too many officials have to be consulted

before specifications for some projects can be drawn up. As a
result, decision-making in relation to important new technological
innovations has been delayed.

Continuing structural problems have been accompanied by familiar
difficulties with goal-setting and attainment. Goals have not been
clarified since hiving off. In spite of the attempt, which we
discussed earlier, to improve the planning capability of the Post
Office no systematic framework for reaching agreement on long-term
objectives and strategy appears to have emerged. Its output goals
are unclear. According to some observers, this is attributable to
defects in the 1969 Act. It is not clear, for example, whether the
Post Office is to be seen as a strictly profit-making organization,
or as one with a responsibility for providing public services
according to social need. It is not known how far efficiency should
be tempered by equity.

System goals are also ill-defined. Indicators of performance
remain rudimentary. Both posts and telecommunications appear to
suffer from the absence of reliable traffic data. The financial
control system essential for accountable management has been
characterized as primitive.

These difficulties have been compounded by role confusion. The
relationships between corporation, sponsoring minister and parliament
are imprecise. The Department of Industry has failed to evaluate
technical projects properly, for example, postal mechanization.
It has failed to subject management policy to systematic review.
This has led to excessively optimistic forecasting. The sponsoring
ministry has, however, intervened in management but in a negative
and inconsistent way. For example, pricing policies have changed
frequently for political rather than commercial reasons. This has
disrupted the continuity of Post Office planning (Corby, 1979).

The organization has also been widely criticized since hiving
off for its increasing insensitivity to environmental pressures.
Customer-corporation relationships have worsened. The corporation
has declined in public estimation. The institutions of the political
environment have proved ineffective in making the corporation
responsive to public opinion. They have presided over a declining
quality of service. Parliamentary scrutiny has proved ineffective.
The Select Committee on Nationalized Industries has been sporadic
in its investigations (Corby, 1979). The users' council appears
to have been co-opted by ministers. The organization's own
marketing capability is extremely weak. These are all indicators
of inflexibility.

ORGANIZATION AND POLITICS

It is assumed that hiving off is a means of insulating an organization
from politics. This is supposed to allow decisions to be based
purely on commercial criteria. It is also designed to permit the
adoption of forms of organization thought impossible in a traditional
department. The case of the Post Office shows that the achievement
of organizational flexibility is neither straightforward nor painless.
Constitutional reform does not necessarily produce behavioural
change.

A second lesson is that political intervention cannot be avoided. If ministers wish to intervene they will not be deterred, in either the scope or nature of their intervention, by the fact that they are dealing with a semi-autonomous agency (NEDO, 1976).

Third, it is questionable whether a public service should be removed from political accountability. The current debate about the status of semi-autonomous agencies as alternatives to government departments focuses on this issue. It questions whether any public function can be considered in exclusively commercial terms. It has drawn attention back to the political values underlying public service provision.

An organizational analysis of government departments must recognize the significance of politics at two levels. There is the level of internal politics among strategic coalitions and competing interests. There is the level of macro-politics concerned with the allocation of societal values. Organizational change can escape neither macro- nor micro-politics when it takes place in the public sector. An approach which ignores the political features of public organizations commits the fallacy of seeking administrative solutions to political problems. The only escape from macro-politics is to define the activity in question as falling outside the public realm. The political significance of such a move is obvious. It will generate political conflict at both levels. Any move to privatize state functions will attract the resistance of groups within and outside affected organizations. Thus organizational change is bound to lead to a heightening of political disputes.

A final lesson of hiving off is that bureaucracy should not be assumed always to be antithetical to democracy. For all its weaknesses bureaucracy remains, as Weber recognized nearly a century ago, an instrument which may be used to ensure the accountability of public servants to elected representatives.

Chapter 7

ALTERNATIVES TO BUREAUCRACY?

Our analysis of departments has shown that like other organizations, they are not to be viewed as harmonious systems in which agreement over means and ends can be taken for granted. We have seen that conflict can arise over goals, structure and technology. The environment, too, is subject to varying interpretations and responses. In contrast the practice of management and reform in government departments (and indeed elsewhere in the public sector) has been dominated by a view - managerialism - which seems to deny this. Much of the theoretical literature on organizations has also characterized them as co-operative social systems. The fact that administrative practice and organisational theorizing are both showing signs of rejecting such an approach is evidence of a changing political and intellectual climate. Managerialism in the 1960s was an optimistic response to problems of performance in public sector organizations. Now we are witnessing a period of disenchantment with the administrative solutions which were sought to political problems.

The managerialist approach to the organization and management of government departments which we described in chapter 5 was part of a much broader view of the political process which dominated British politics in the 1950s and 1960s. This interpretation of politics has been dubbed by Trevor Smith as 'consensual technocracy'. It dates from a period of marked decline in conventional party politics associated with a widespread view that 'post-industrial' society had witnessed the 'end of ideology'. Class conflict and ideological dispute were regarded as redundant. 'Social engineering, piecemeal reform, or incrementalism resulting from the bargaining of interest groups (reflecting divisions of status rather than those of class), together with the application of new skills and techniques would determine the content of public policy' (T. Smith, 1972b, p.307; see also 1972a). Widespread agreement about the basic rules of political life was said to underlie the nation's political stability. Consensus was said to exist on the desirable nature, pace and method of political change. There was an assumption in political circles that a lack of profound ideological conflict over the nature of society and the economy, combined with a high level of confidence in and respect for British political arrangements had led to both procedural and substantive consensus (B. Smith, 1976, pp.31-2).

There are hints in recent political events that consensus in British politics is not as strong as it was. The major political parties are becoming ideologically more polarized. The territorial integrity of the state has been threatened, at least momentarily, in pressures for devolution. Political life seems more and more to be dominated by industrial conflict. The police appear to respond more violently to dissent. The Northern Ireland problem seems to have defeated those searching for a political solution. The electorate has become more volatile and disillusioned with politics and politicians. The judiciary has been drawn into industrial disputes.

While it is unlikely that such developments represent a fundamental breakdown of the political system, it is evident that managerialism, or consensual technocracy, has suffered a considerable blow. Few people now would place much confidence in the reform of institutions and administrative processes after the experience of local government and Health Service reorganization. The Fulton reforms, though profound from a narrow internal perspective, have had no noticeable effect on administrative performance. The 'reform' of parliament has left relations between legislature and executive unaltered. Civil service power, relative to that of elected representatives, is as great as ever. In political circles institutional panaceas seem feeble and irrelevant when set against the problems of inflation, unemployment, productivity, the balance of payments and economic growth which impinge on every family every day.

Political disillusionment with managerialism has been accompanied by the formulation of theories which perceive organizations internally as political systems. Radical writers also see wider political problems as deriving from the organizational characteristics of contemporary society. The solutions which present themselves involve fundamental organizational change requiring either alternative organizations or even alternatives to organizations. Whereas managerialism left the basic framework of political assumptions intact, recent theorists see organizational change as a precursor to more fundamental political reforms. Radical organizational change for them is part of a wider realignment of power in society.

One response to the failure of managerialism is the idea of governmental 'overload', the view that administrative failure is due to the excessive burden of tasks which the state has assumed. The idea of 'overload' or 'ungovernability' suggests a system of government confronted with seemingly insuperable problems.

The blame for the fact that the business of government appears to have become more difficult is put first on the growth of government and second, on the declining capacity of governments to perform their chosen tasks efficiently or even effectively: 'just as the range of responsibilities of Governments has increased, so, to a large extent independently, their capacity to exercise their responsibilities has declined' (King, 1975, p.288). The main reason for governmental failure is the number of dependency relationships that contemporary governments are required to enter into. In addition, the likelihood of compliance from those on whom modern governments depend for the successful achievement of their objectives has declined. Governments are merely participants in complex processes of bargaining with pressure groups, industry international bodies and professional associations. The possible consequences of overload are a fall in the level of legitimacy accruing to government and greater internal complexity in the governmental machine. Indeed, since it is thought unlikely that the grasp of government can be strengthened it is unavoidable that its reach should be shortened. Dependency is unlikely to decrease. Compliance is unlikely to increase. The lesson for theorists of administration is obvious. Rather than trying to improve the performance of government along managerialist lines, 'they should be concerned more with how the number of tasks that government has come to be expected to perform can be reduced' (King, 1975, p.296).

Dissatisfaction with managerialism has taken a different form elsewhere. It has been challenged in the United States, where it has had a long history, by a group known as the 'New Public Administration' (Marini, 1971). This is a loose coalition of academics and practitioners, formed in 1968, which has asserted, contrary to conventional opinion, the political and human signifi-cance of administration. They acknowledge the harmful effects of the administrative state and argue for its dismantling. They castigate the domination of American society by bureaucratic forms of rule. Government has become bureaucratic in the sense of rule by officials operating in alliance with special interests rather than in pursuit of the public interest. Indeed, it is seen as an alliance with precisely those interests which already enjoy a disproportionate degree of power and resources to the neglect of wider social needs.

The internal characteristics of public bureaucracies are inextricably interwoven into their political functions. Change is needed to make these organizations less oppressive, not only to those working in them but also to those members of society brought into contact with them. Basically this entails making them less authoritarian. They should become more humane for their members and 'responsive to the need to redress social misery and advance the human condition generally' (Savage, 1974, p.153). Public organizations should become more participative, democratic, client-oriented, decentralized and adaptive. Academics and practitioners should move away from problem solving in support of the establish-ment, and towards the development of vision, leadership and intellectual vitality on behalf of the disadvantaged.

NPA thus hopes to link 'scholarship to moral purpose to help achieve the ideals of genuine grassroots democracy and the extension of human freedom' (Savage, 1974, p.154). It accords to public administration goals of the highest ethical order: the reduction of economic, social and even psychic suffering; the enhancement of life opportunities for organizational members and clients alike; and the pursuit of social equity. The challenge of this school of thought is to a system of administration which seeks efficiency regardless of the goals to be achieved. NPA elevates ethical and political outcomes of administrative action to a position of pre-eminence.

An alternative approach to the organization of the future is to predict the death of bureaucracy (recommending its demise at the same time). This has been a familiar theme of recent writings on organizational change. Part of this approach to the future is optimistic, suggesting non-bureaucratic alternatives; part is nihilistic, predicting an unorganized future. The remedial approach, very much associated with the early writings of Warren Bennis (for example, 1969), finds bureaucracy wanting in its inability to cope with tension between managerial and individual goals. It dehumanizes those condemned to work within it. It finds difficulty in adapting to a changing environment, especially one in which personal allegiance to hierarchical organizations loses its attraction. The hierarchical form of authority, it is argued, is becoming increasingly incompatible with a felt need for more democratic lifestyles. It is even argued that democratic forms of human association are more effective in coping with change, since they embody principles essential for the adaptive organization such as freedom of communication, the authority of expertise rather than office, and the search for consensus. Democracy also gives the organization a human bias. All this is reflected in the 'organizational development' movement which attempts to revitalize organizations through the abandonment of authoritarian procedures and the instituting of collegiate relationships.

The radical denunciation of organizations is associated with the writings of Ivan Illich (for example, 1973). Here we have a revolt against organizations of all types, public and private. They no longer serve the interests of either individual or community. They constitute a threat to morality itself. They are technically rational only in the sense that they can satisfy the needs which they themselves have artificially created. By renouncing the autonomy of the individual in favour of management by others they heighten alienation, obstruct 'conviviality' and make man the victim of 'treatment' by professionals and bureaucrats. The individual's true needs are subverted. His wants and desires are created and managed by others. Progress from alienation to autonomy can only occur if society is deliberately 'de-organized'.

The remedial and radical approaches have a number of ideas in common: impatience with hierarchy and specialization; hostility to the sublimation of personal goals; a concern with the promotion of 'authentic' human needs; a strong moral and humanistic dimension; and a renunciation of alienation. Where they differ is in the confidence placed in the rationality of organizations and in their view of the success of organizations in coping with the environment. While the remedial account sees organizations as failing to respond to a dynamic environment the radical critique sees the problem as one of institutional growth and success and the need to return to a simpler form of life in which organizations become redundant.

Taken together, these critiques appear threatening to the kinds of organization we are familiar with in the public sector and in particular the government department. Though they display differing ideological preconceptions, they all constitute an attack on prevailing bureaucratic modes of organization. Yet they are not entirely convincing in the solutions that they offer to the dilemmas which they perceive in an organizational society.

The problem with the ungovernability thesis is that off-loading the functions of the state is even more difficult than hiving off

functions to different kinds of state agency. This is a highly
political solution likely to generate political opposition. The
state is hardly likely to gain credibility in the eyes of those it
has made dependent on it (the unemployed, pensioners, the poor,
unviable companies and so on) if they are now told to go it alone.
To argue that the only objective in reducing the reach of government
is to increase its 'grasp' in the sense of making it more efficient
is to perpetuate the technocratic approach. Even if it could be
shown that performance could be improved by reducing the scope of
government, it is another matter altogether to show that other
values, such as accountability, participation, responsiveness or
decentralization will be enhanced by a reduction in quantity. Nor
can we ignore the substance of governmental intervention when
deciding what to cut out or whether the private sector will provide
services which might not be profitable.   Different political
interests will want the state to shed different things. Not all
will approve of unloading profitable state enterprises, for example.

The recognition by the New Public Administration of the political
significance of administrative processes in which political problems
and solutions are increasingly framed, is indisputably a necessary
feature of administrative analysis. No one would dispute the
importance of relating administration to the play of power in
society and the formation of policy in government. We ourselves
have noted the indivisibility of politics and administration. Nor
would those with a social conscience find much fault with the
ethical ideals behind NPA. But the movement's credibility declines
if the political logic of the argument is pursued further. Can a
democratic society tolerate its bureaucrats monopolizing political
decision-making even if they are motivated by the highest ideals?
And what guarantee is there that bureaucrats can be selected and
socialized to pursue the goals of the good society? The NPA has
been praised for its political awareness, yet its political analysis
hardly seems to go far enough. No reason is given for expecting that
the political system will be either prepared to produce, or indeed
be capable of producing a new breed of administrator. Without a
fundamental restructuring of the economic and social order it is
unlikely that a different type of administrator will be recruited,
with different ideals and objectives. And it would be surprising
if the dominant political interests permitted even the most
enlightened administrators to initiate new policies in pursuit of
social justice, equality and economic opportunity. The New Public
Administration exaggerates the options open to public servants
within a particular socio-economic structure.

The death of bureaucracy approach exaggerates the freedom
available in contemporary society to move to a non-organizational
future. It underestimates the difficulties inherent in such an
exercise and under-emphasizes many positive organizational values.
The first defect in this thinking lies in its presentation of a
primitive model of bureaucracy. This is characterized as an
organization perpetually out of alignment with changing technologies
and environments. Bureaucracy is seen as inherently inflexible.
As our earlier analysis shows this is extremely unsophisticated.
Public sector bureaucracies are able not only to respond to
change. They may, in addition, be responsible for initiating change.

They have often innovated in fields such as scientific research,
social policy and economic planning. The technological and scientific
changes which are said to confound bureaucracies or be suppressed
by them are often produced by those bureaucratic forms of organization
themselves.

Second, a changing environment may require a stable system of
rules and control. Members of organizations need rules and hierarchy
for the same reason as clients: they guarantee consistency and
predictability rather than arbitrary power. A bureaucratic form of
organization may be in line with technology and environment when they
are stable. A group of organizations labelled bureaucratic may
differ from each other in shape and design. Their bureaucratic
features vary. They display different degrees of hierarchy,
specialization, procedural regularity and so on. Such variability
may reflect the particular tasks that each has to perform. Third,
the model of man implied in the anti-organization writings underestimates the capabilities of people to bargain, calculate and
negotiate in defence of their interests: 'anti-bureaucratic writing
often employs a unitary rather than pluralistic model of the social
structure of the organization' (Pitt, 1979, p.12). While some
members of organizations may be intent on introducing organic
working procedures others will be equally committed to preserving
bureaucratic features. In addition a naive and simplistic model of
human motivation is offered. A bureaucratic structure is assumed
to be inimical to individual self-actualization. Key issues are
overlooked in this approach. Is a view of man as 'inexhaustively
creative' particularly convincing? Many individuals within
organizations have 'renounced self-actualization as a behavioural
strategy preferring instead quietism and routine' (Pitt, 1979, p.13).
Bureaucracy is a means of guaranteeing both. Assuming people wish
to self-actualize, bureaucracy sets proper limits to the freedom
of members to pursue their own goals at the expense of others.
It also limits the organization's freedom to define goals for itself
at variance with those of elected governments.

Finally, there is the problem of guaranteeing that the clients
which organizations, especially those of government, exist to serve
will be protected in any future unorganized society. The vacuums
created by abandoning organizations are likely to be filled by
social arrangements from which the weak and deprived can expect
little protection. This recalls a problem with the ungovernability
thesis. It seems naively apolitical to assume that organization
will not be needed in the creation of freedom and justice, a central
concern of the New Public Administration.

Disenchantment with bureaucracy is nothing new. It is a
quintessentially paradoxical phenomenon. It has costs and benefits
for a democratic political system. Bureaucracy can act on behalf
of exploitation and oppression. It can prove efficient for
politically suspect objectives as well as politically desirable.
Concern about the negative attributes of bureaucracy generally
neglects its positive features. A political approach to bureaucracy
highlights this dilemma. People have investments in it. This
not only includes officials and politicians wishing to make economic
and industrial advances, provide public goods or pursue sectional
interests. It includes a whole range of social groups who benefit

from services provided by bureaucratic organizations. Remove
organization and the individual is vulnerable to more sinister forces.
   To understand the nature of organizational society in the future
requires a political model. This is necessary if internal structure
is to be comprehended, particularly in times of change. It is also
relevant to understanding organizations in their broader social
setting. Organizational analysis teaches us that organizations are
not simply instruments in which agreement over goals is taken for
granted. Neither are they simple based on the notions of efficiency
and rationality. Rather they are to be seen as structures of control
in which the choices of key decision makers reflect conflicting
values and interests (Salaman, 1979, p.28). Such theories of the
relationship between power in society and power in organizations
point to the ideological qualities of organizational life. We must
ask: efficient for whom and for what? The development of this
approach constitutes an attack on existing managerialist assumptions
about harmony, mutual interest and administrative neutrality (Clegg
and Dunkerley, 1980).
   What this demonstrates is that an administrative science of
bureaucracy needs to be augmented by a political theory of organization. Organization theory appears to be moving in this direction.
The conceptual apparatus of political theory must be relevant to
both the internal functioning of organizations and to their relationships within their social and political environment. Rights,
obligations and liberties are increasingly defined for us by our
involvement with organizations as members and clients. The role
of bureaucracy in a democratic political system presents a conflict
between the power of officials and the power of the people or their
elected representatives. Furthermore the inherently oligarchic
nature of organizations, based on differential levels of authority
and unequal rights of decision-making, conflicts with the principles
of a democratic society which assume an equality of individual
worth. It is important to distinguish between questions about the
structure of organizations and questions concerning who controls
them, the uses to which they are put and the values which they
serve. A central issue for the new political theory of organizations
must be the paradox of bureaucracy. Antithetical to some human
values, such as responsiveness, accessibility and sensitivity, it
is supportive of others such as accountability, rationality and
equity, of central significance to a democratic system of government.

BIBLIOGRAPHY

BAKER, R.J.S. (1972), 'Administrative Theory and Public Administration', Hutchinson, London.
BALOGH, T. (1959), The apotheosis of the dilettante, in H. Thomas (ed.), 'The Establishment', Anthony Blond, London.
BEALEY, F. (1976), 'The Post Office Engineering Union', Bachman & Turner, London.
BENNIS, W. (1969), Beyond bureaucracy, in A. Etzioni (ed.), 'Readings on Modern Organizations', Prentice Hall, Englewood Cliffs, NJ.
BENNIS, W. (1970), A funny thing happened on the way to the future, 'American Psychologist', vol.25, no.7.
BLAU, P.M. and SCOTT, W.R. (1963), 'Formal Organizations. A Comparative Approach', Routledge & Kegan Paul, London.
BRADLEY, D. and WILKIE, R. (1974), 'The Concept of Organization', Blackie, Glasgow.
BRIDGES, LORD (1964), 'The Treasury', Allen & Unwin, London.
BROWN, R.G.S. and STEEL, D.R. (1979), 'The Administrative Process in Britain', 2nd edition, Methuen, London.
BURNS, T. and STALKER, G.M. (1961), 'The Management of Innovation', Tavistock, London.
CARTER COMMITTEE (1977), 'Report of the Post Office Review Committee', Cmnd 6850, HMSO, London.
CHAPMAN, B. (1963), 'British Government Observed', Allen & Unwin, London.
CHAPMAN, L. (1979), 'Your Disobedient Servant. The Continuing Story of Whitehall's Overspending', 2nd edition, Penguin, Harmondsworth.
CHILD, J. (1972), Organizational structures, environment and performance: the role of strategic choice, 'Sociology', vol.6, no.1.
CHILD, J. and MANSFIELD, R. (1972), Technology, size and organization structure, 'Sociology', vol.6, no.3, September-December.
CLEGG, S. and DUNKERLEY, D. (1980), 'Organization, Class and Control', Routledge & Kegan Paul, London.
COOPER, K. (1975), Accountability in government: the Employment Service Agency, 'Public Administration Bulletin', no.19, December.
CORBY, M. (1979), 'The Postal Business 1969-79. A Study in Public Sector Management', Kogan Page, London.
CROZIER, M. (1964), 'The Bureaucratic Phenomenon', Tavistock, London.

DAWSON, S. (1979), Organizational analysis and the study of policy formulation and implementation, 'Public Administration Bulletin', no.31, December.
DRUCKER, P.F. (1968), 'The Practice of Management', Pan, London.
ETZIONI, A. (1961), 'A Comparative Analysis of Complex Organizations', Free Press, New York.
ETZIONI, A. (1964), 'Modern Organizations', Prentice Hall, Englewood Cliffs, NJ.
FABIAN SOCIETY (1964), 'The Administrators', London.
FAYOL, H. (1949), 'General Industrial Management', Pitman, London.
FOX, A. (1966), 'Industrial Sociology and Industrial Relations', Research Paper no.3, Royal Commission on Trade Unions and Employers' Associations, HMSO, London.
FULTON, LORD (1968), 'The Civil Service', Report of the Committee 1966-68 (Chairman Lord Fulton), Cmnd 3638, HMSO, London.
GARRETT, J. (1972), 'The Management of Government', Penguin, Harmondsworth.
HAILSHAM, LORD (1978), 'The Dilemma of Democracy', Collins, London.
HALL, R.H. (1974), 'Organizations. Structure and Process', Prentice Hall International, London.
HANSON, A.H. and WALLES, M. (1975), 'Governing Britain. A Guidebook to Political Institutions', 2nd edition, Fontana Collins, London.
HECLO, H., and WILDAVSKY, A. (1974), 'The Private Government of Public Money', Macmillan, London.
HEWART, LORD JUSTICE, (1929), 'The New Despotism', Ernest Benn, London.
HILL, M.J. (1972), 'The Sociology of Public Administration', Weidenfeld & Nicolson, London.
HININGS, C.R. and GREENWOOD, R. (1973), Research into local government reorganization, 'Public Administration Bulletin', no.15, December.
HOOD, C., DUNSIRE, A. and THOMPSON, S. (1979), Describing the status quo in Whitehall: a prerequisite for the analysis of change, 'Public Administration Bulletin', no.31, December.
ILLICH, I. (1973), 'Tools for Conviviality', Calder & Boyars, London.
JORDAN, G. (1976), Hiving off and departmental agencies, 'Public Administration Bulletin', no.21, August.
KEELING, D. (1972), 'Management in Government', Allen & Unwin, London.
KING, A. (1975), Overload: problems of governing in the 1970's, 'Political Studies', vol.23, nos.2-3, June-September.
LAWRENCE, P.R. and LORSCH, J.W. (1967), 'Organization and Environment, Managing Differentiation and Integration', Harvard University Press, Boston.
MARINI, F. (ed.) (1971), 'Toward a New Public Administration. The Minnowbrook Perspective', Chandler Publishing, Scranton.
MERTON, R. (1940), Bureaucratic structure and personality, 'Social Forces', vol.17, pp.560-8.
MICHELS, R. (1915), 'Political Parties', Collier, 1962 edition, New York.
NATIONAL WHITLEY COUNCIL (1975), 'Civil Servants and Change', Civil Service Department, London.
NEDO (1976), 'A Study of UK Nationalized Industries, Their role in the economy and control in the future', National Economic Development Office, London.

NISKANEN, W.A. (1973), 'Bureaucracy: Servant or Master?', Hobart
Paper, Institute of Economic Affairs, London.
PARKER, R.S. and SUBRAMANIAM, V. (1964), Public and Private
Administration, 'International Review of Administrative Sciences',
vol.30, no.4.
PARSONS, T. (1960), 'Structure and Process in Modern Societies',
Free Press, Glencoe, Illinois.
PERROW, C. (1970), 'Organizational Analysis. A Sociological View',
Tavistock, London.
PERROW, C. (1972), 'Complex Organizations. A Critical Essay',
Scott Foresman, Glenview, Illinois.
PITT, D.C. (1979), The end of bureaucracy: the beginning of ideology?,
'Public Administration Bulletin', no.31, December.
PITT, D.C. (1980), 'The Telecommunications Function in the British
Post Office. A Case Study of Bureaucratic Adaptation', Saxon House,
Farnborough.
PLOWDEN COMMITTEE (1961), 'Report of the Committee on the Control
of Public Expenditure', Cmnd 1432, HMSO, London.
PUGH, D.S., HICKSON, D.J., HININGS, C.R. and TURNER, C. (1968),
Dimensions of organization structure, 'Administrative Science
Quarterly', vol.13, no.1.
PUGH, D.S., HICKSON, D.J., HININGS, C.R. and TURNER, C. (1969),
The context of organization structures, 'Administrative Science
Quarterly', vol.14, no.1.
RICHARDSON, J.J. and JORDAN, A.G. (1979), 'Governing under Pressure.
The Policy Process in a Post-Parliamentary Democracy', Martin
Robertson, Oxford.
ROBINSON, H. (1948), 'The British Post Office', Princeton University
Press.
ROSE, M. (1978), 'Industrial Behaviour. Theoretical Development
since Taylor', Penguin, Harmondsworth.
SALAMAN, G. (1979), 'Work Organizations. Resistance and Control',
Longman, London.
SAVAGE, P. (1974), Dismantling the administrative state: paradigm
reformulation of public administration, 'Political Studies', vol.22,
no.2, June.
SELECT COMMITTEE ON ESTIMATES (1958), 'Treasury Control of
Expenditure', Sixth Report, 1957-8, HC 254, HMSO, London.
SELECT COMMITTEE ON ESTIMATES (1965), 'Recruitment to the Civil
Service', Sixth Report, 1964-5 session, HC 308, HMSO, London.
SHARP, E. (1969), 'The Ministry of Housing and Local Government',
Allen & Unwin, London.
SILLS, D.L. (1957), 'The Volunteers', Free Press, Chicago.
SILVERMAN, D. (1970), 'The Theory of Organizations. A Sociological
Framework', Heinemann, London.
SMITH, B. (1976), 'Policy Making in British Government. An Analysis
of Power and Rationality', Martin Robertson, London.
SMITH, T. (1972a), 'Anti-politics: Consensus, Reform and Protest
in Britain', Charles Knight, London.
SMITH, T. (1972b), Protest and democracy, in R. Benewick and T. Smith
(eds), 'Direct Action and Democratic Politics', Allen & Unwin,
London.
SMITH, T. (1979), 'The Politics of the Corporate Economy', Martin
Robertson, Oxford.

STANYER, J. and SMITH, B.C. (1976), 'Administering Britain', Fontana, London.

STEWART, R. (1967), 'The Reality of Management', Pan, London.

STRAUSS, A., et al. (1973), The hospital and its negotiated order, in G. Salaman and K. Thompson (eds), 'People and Organizations', Longman, London.

VROOM, V.H. and DECI, E.L. (1970), 'Management and Motivation', Penguin, Harmondsworth.

WEBER, M. (1947), 'The Theory of Social and Economic Organization', Oxford University Press.

WHITE PAPER (1970), 'The Reorganization of Central Government', Cmnd 4506, HMSO, London.

WILLIAMS, M. (1972), 'Inside Number 10', Weidenfeld & Nicolson, London.

WOOD, S. (1979), A reappraisal of the contingency approach to organization, 'Journal of Management Studies', vol.16, no.3, October.

WOODWARD, J. (1965), 'Industrial Organization: Theory and Practice', Oxford University Press, London.

WRIGHT, M. (1980), Growth, restraint and rationality, in M. Wright (ed.), 'Public Spending Decisions. Growth and Restraint in the 1970's', Allen & Unwin, London.

INDEX